CELTIC BRITAIN

WITH 133 ILLUSTRATIONS, 9 IN COLOUR

CHARLES THOMAS

Celtic Britain

THAMES AND HUDSON

THIS IS VOLUME ONE HUNDRED AND THREE IN THE SERIES
Ancient Peoples and Places
GENERAL EDITOR: GLYN DANIEL

Half-title page: Chi-rho, with flanking alpha and omega,
from a silver bowl, Water Newton hoard, early 4th century.

Title pages: The Mounth – the range of high ground intersected
with passes that, for centuries, divided northern Caledonians and
Picts from their southern compatriots.

Text and monochrome illustrations printed in Great Britain
by BAS Printers Ltd, Over Wallop, Hampshire
Colour illustrations printed in Great Britain
by George Over Limited, Rugby, Warwickshire
Bound in Great Britain by the Bath Press, Bath

Contents

Preface

'PRESUMPTION OR MEANNESS are both too often the only articles to be found in a preface', wrote the poet George Crabbe. So spiky a sentiment would have come better from Crabbe's friend Dr Samuel Johnson, but it contains a truth that archaeologists and historians alike should consider. It *is* presumptuous to suppose that in the 1980s any one small book can do justice to so vast a topic as Celtic Britain. Here, I restrict this title to the Celtic-speaking regions of north and west Britain (excluding Ireland) as they were between the Romans and the Norsemen, approximately the 5th to early 8th centuries AD. Nora Chadwick's predecessor volume of the same title in this series, published in 1963, took a broader view that harmonized with her own immensely gifted, humanistic and very broad approach; much that she chose to include belongs, on a strict interpretation, to Viking and post-Viking times. In the last quarter-century there has been both a veritable explosion of knowledge (in this period as in most temporal divisions of British archaeology) and a greatly enhanced interest displayed by a new generation of scholars. To cover all the ground mapped out by Nora Chadwick would require a book too long and too detailed to reach the general reader. I write therefore instead in slighter vein, trying to keep the text within the bounds of place and time already mentioned. For me as for Mrs Chadwick the general reader is all-important. He or she on both sides of the Atlantic, and elsewhere, may be the informed student, the college or university beginner, the enthusiast for further education or simply the person who wants to make the effort to find out.

But to find out what? Since 1963, and much more so than in the preceding post-War decades, the 'Celtic' side of Britain has frequently occupied the front of the stage. At the most obvious there has been – there still is – the whole matter of Northern Ireland, where British politicians face the problems of reconciling results of a distant part-Celtic migration, from Protestant Lowland Scotland to Catholic Ulster. For reasons that are mostly socio-economic and that I cannot pretend to be able to explain, the reassertion of regional identities within Britain reached a temporary peak in the 1970s and did so in a wholly Celtic guise: pressure for Scottish and Welsh devolution. The Welsh language rightly refuses to lie down and die, the Isle of Man produced an underground organization dedicated to ridding Man of rich English settlers and in my native Cornwall the drive to learn, teach and publish in revived Cornish has grown from a hobby to an industry.

Now all this may be of great interest, if not commonplace, to full-time Celtic scholars or students, but the general reader is wholly entitled to ask why this Celtic element persists, and where and whence it arose, and it would be extremely difficult to answer all that satisfactorily in a sentence. Accordingly I have done my best to isolate a period in Britain's past where, and possibly where alone, the seeds of the present were sown.

To claim that the past completely shapes the present would be as dangerous as to suppose that studies of past and present give complete guidelines for the future; there are far too many variables and human history does not seem to be predetermined. But one is bound to suspect that many people in Britain – certainly in England – and even more people in other English-speaking countries are told or taught far less about the Celts than about Anglo-Saxons, Normans, Plantagenets and Tudors. Almost all Welsh people speak and write English with total fluency. Hardly any English people can read or correctly pronounce a word of Welsh! It would indeed be a presumption if I were to pose as an expert interpreter of one component of the British nation to another, but throughout this book I have done my best, deliberately, to relate the past to the present and then leave the reader to make his or her assessment of the link between them.

As for Crabbe's warning about meanness in a preface, I can gladly avoid this by a blanket acknowledgment to my colleagues, past students and friends, genuinely too numerous to be listed individually, whose researches and publications provide the basis for my selective and personal view. Most of them are named in the Select Bibliography at the end. As archaeology and early history continue to spawn more and more intricate books and articles, the task of the synthesist is made no easier but it decidedly becomes more necessary. Nora Chadwick spent her working life encouraging others to replace and to update what she herself had written. No statement about Celtic Britain can or should be more than a stop-gap, but I shall be more than rewarded if this one serves for a few years.

Colour plates   I Tintagel, on the north Cornish coast – perhaps a royal seat of the Celtic kingdom of Dumnonia.
II A gold buckle, 5 cm high, from the spectacular pagan hoard deposited by a merchant or jeweller in the late 4th century, and discovered in 1979 near Thetford, Norfolk. Many of the objects are dedicated to the god Faunus; here a satyr holding grapes faces two horses' heads which form a hinge.
III The recently discovered hanging-bowl (diameter c.24 cm) from St Paul in the Bail, Lincoln. Note the two escutcheons (strengthening plates) joining the loops to the bowl.
IV Enamelled mount (diameter 5.5 cm) from the base of a hanging-bowl; from the Sutton Hoo ship burial, 7th century.
V The most famous portable reliquary or 'house-shaped shrine': the Monymusk Reliquary. Of late 7th- or early 8th-century date, and perhaps Scottish in origin, it is only 105 mm across, with gilt and silver ornaments on wood, and may have housed a relic of St Columba.

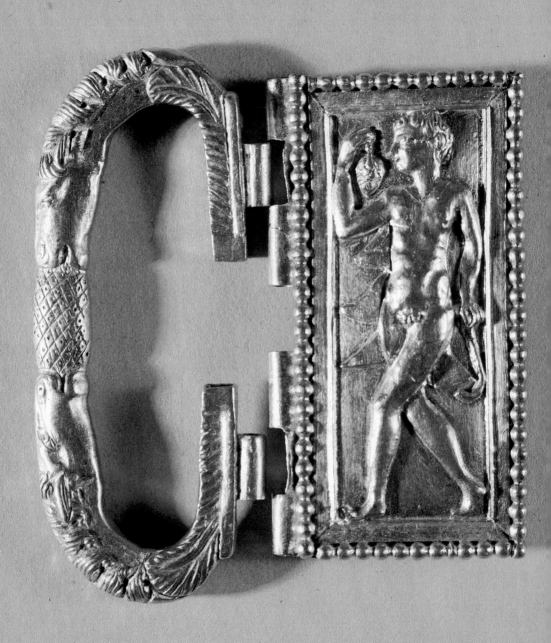

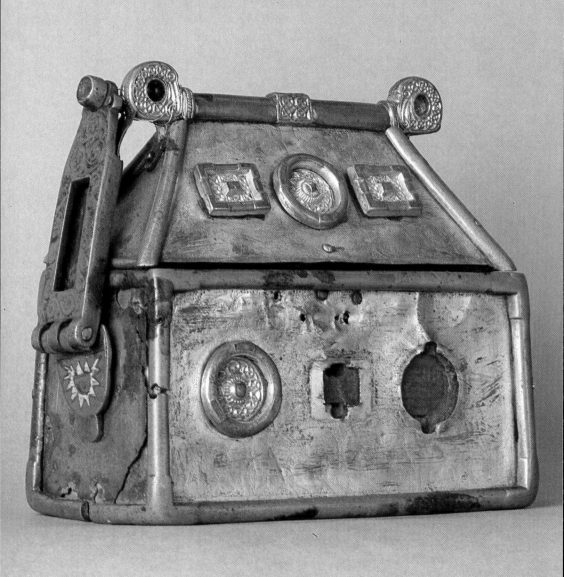

1 · Introduction: Celtic Britain today

T
HOSE OF US who habitually travel around Great Britain would do
well to pause occasionally and to take a hard look at the road signs
and the boards on our remaining railway stations. In its European
and American guises, English may be a world language, and place-names
such as Newtown, Grange-over-Sands, Ashford and Bridgwater in
theory intelligible to, for instance, an English-speaking Belgian – at any
rate, to one who knows that a *grange* was originally a large arable farm
with its dwellings and outbuildings. But a knowledge of this scope is of no
use when gazing at signposts that read *Penhalurick* $1\frac{1}{2}$, or *Footpath to Na
Gruagaichean*, or *Knock-y-doonee*. How is one meant to pronounce
Llanfihangel-uwch-gwili (a village near Carmarthen), or the name of that
excessive and much photographed Anglesey railway halt, Llanfair-
pwllgwyngyllgogerychwyndrobwillantysiliogogogoch? Does this gib-
berish mean anything, and how do people manage to talk in a language
of which large chunks appear to be devoid of the normal European
vowels? Why is there still so much of this un-Englishness on display in
Britain?

The clue lies buried in the word Britain itself, something that has
never meant the same as England. Accidents of history have placed the
metropolitan capital at London, instead of Bristol or Edinburgh. The
British may not be as *centraliste* as the French with their Buonapartist
legacy, but the almost universal misuse of 'English' to convey the
meaning 'British' overlooks from a southeast English standpoint the fact
that majorities in Wales and Scotland would not dream of calling
themselves anything other than Welsh or Scottish. There are also plenty
of Cornish and Manx to support them in this practice. The English,
heaven knows, should find enough problems in defining their own
identity without seeking to extend it to other peoples'. They were early
enriched by Scandinavian immigrants, then by Normans and other
varieties of Frenchmen, and more recently by significant Flemish,
Jewish, Italian, Polish and Chinese infusions. Even the English language
proves to be dualistic and inconsistent. 'The hound ran along quickly
behind the wagon' is a sentence all of whose words come straight from the
Anglo-Saxon or Old English of a thousand years past. Yet one can also
say this in words – real English words – taken from Latin: 'The domestic
canine quadruped progressed at a superior velocity in a position anterior
to the vehicle motivated by dual equine traction.'

Any historian of Britain, if he or she stops to think about this, ought to face a battery of the most awkward questions. A small country, subjected over several millennia to prehistoric farming and clearance, and the home of about a million or so people, was conquered in AD 43 by the expanding Roman empire. For nearly four centuries it was then incorporated within the western part of that empire; in fact, it *was* Roman. Britannia, as the Romans called it, was ruled not so much by the legionaries' swords as by a complex bureaucracy, unending taxation, a sequence of Mediterranean-based religions culminating in Christianity and above all by the Latin language. Why then do I write, and you read, in a tongue that I can set out in a form which is not that of the speech of old Rome and where no word need have more than one short part, or can alternatively precipitate itself dramatically into polysyllabic metamorphosis? If we think of the linguistic histories of France, Belgium (in part), Spain, Portugal, Sardinia, Italy and Romania, why are we not conversing in something demonstrably descended from Vulgar or popularly spoken Latin?

If this book provides no simple answer, it is because none exists. In the period from about AD 100 to 500 a great many ordinary people in Britain *did* speak a simplified conversational Latin, regardless of whether by birth they were British, European, North African or western Asiatic. Latin was the sole compulsory language of the military and the machinery of government. This we can comprehend; it had to be, just as in India the British were obliged to govern through English and to a lesser extent Urdu, a Hindustani camp-language promoted within a multilingual army. But Latin was also used to write rude words on the walls of Romano-British public conveniences and brothels, for price tickets and warehouse tallies, and in letters home from frozen mercenaries asking their loved ones to hurry up and send some woollen underpants.

Largely, this refers to what is today England. In Scotland, much of Wales and the deep southwest, if people could speak Latin at all their first tongues were the progressively evolved forms of what had been used before the Roman conquest. It is actually remarkable that in the 1980s Welsh, a complex written and spoken language, goes back directly to the British language spoken (though not written) in the same region in the AD 80s. As George Orwell might have put it, all those in Britain are British, but some are more British than others.

The next conquest of Britain, which was not a single intentional episode as Rome's had been, occurred at irregular stages during the 5th to 7th centuries AD. The peoples we know for convenience as Anglo-Saxons came thereby to dominate England. In the 7th century they were converted piecemeal to Christianity – not by the native Britons, many of whom *were* Christian, but from the Continent and in a roundabout way from Ireland and the Irish colonies in western Britain, whose own Christianity was partly derived from late Roman Britain, partly inspired by European contact. In England the regional dialects of the native Late

1 The major kingdoms and place-names mentioned in the text.

British, and any spoken Latin, were mostly superseded by regional dialects of Anglo-Saxon. Power, arms, land, wealth, and then learning, art and literature passed to the dominant English. The rise of the kingdoms of Mercia, and Wessex (setting of the national hero King Alfred), the concentration of royal courts in the south with their correspondingly easier contact with Europe, and the resuscitation of southern Roman cities like Canterbury, Winchester and London all led to a southern dialect of Middle English forming the basis of standard Modern English. Happily this has never eclipsed all the old regional forms. Nor will it, as long as English dialects persist, and as long as Robert Burns can find readers in Scotland (and Moscow). Had Anglo-Saxon power remained after the 7th century in the north, York or Newcastle would be the national capital; and a sentence like, 'Which one of you would go with him that night?', might well have been standardized as *Quilk yin o ye wad gang wi him that nicht?*

Returning from what might have been to what decidedly is, note that the homeland of Standard English is a geopolitical complexity that few of its inhabitants, and even fewer foreigners, fully grasp. The term 'the British Isles', all those lying northwest of and divided by sea from the European continent, includes Britain itself, with the northern archipelagos of Orkney and Shetland – pledged to the Scottish crown in 1468–69 by King Christian I of Norway and Denmark and annexed to Scotland by an act of the Scottish Parliament in 1471. It must also cover Ireland, now for the greater part a sovereign independent republic, Eire, under its constitution of 1937; and in a strictly geographical interpretation the Faeroes, an outlying part of the kingdom of Denmark 200 miles northwest from Shetland.

The United Kingdom (of Great Britain and Northern Ireland) means England, Wales and Scotland together with the Isle of Man, which passed from the Scandinavian to the Scottish crown in 1226, thence to Edward III of England in 1334, and is now a Crown dependency, a kind of sub-kingdom; Northern Ireland, or those six Irish counties which under the 1921 Government of Ireland Act were granted a particular status and thus excluded from the Irish Free State and the subsequent Republic; and the Channel Islands, *Les Iles Anglo-Normandes*. Geographically again these last are part of France but, as the remnants of William the Conqueror's Duchy of Normandy, form a dependency of the British Crown, in respect of which the Queen is also Duchess of Normandy.

In the sense followed here, Britain is the unitary and largest island (which thus excludes Ireland). 'Celtic Britain' is a permissible association because, taking area alone, England makes up no more than 56 per cent of Britain. The adjective Celtic means, in the strict and most pedantic form, 'of or pertaining to the Celtic group of Indo-European languages'. It has long been extended to embrace virtually everything connected with past and present peoples, inhabiting lands where a Celtic language is or was or is thought to have been current.

We shall meet the Celtic British language again in the next chapter. All that need be said here is that a hypothetical Common Celtic had emerged by 1000 BC from Indo-European, and that from about the 6th century BC its speakers, under various names, were known to the Greeks and then to the Romans as the dominant peoples of central and western Europe. At a later but still prehistoric phase, Common Celtic became divided into Q-Celtic and P-Celtic, according to which branch of it preserved or else changed to p an initial sound that can be written as q^u or k^w. The main problem, which we shall not pursue, is that the oldest identifiable forms of Celtic spoken in most of Ireland were Q-Celtic; whereas in Britain, where our earliest information begins around 300 BC with names recorded by Greek travellers and explorers, the language was equally clearly P-Celtic. In both cases it must be supposed that Celtic was introduced by settlers from the Continent. Obviously, then, either different sources or different dates have to be involved. The weight of present opinion favours a loose notion of Q-Celtic speakers reaching Ireland rather before 500 BC, with the majority of P-Celtic speakers reaching Britain somewhat later. The reader is warned that there are other opinions, but a full recital would occupy most of this book.

The Irish language, having gone through its Primitive, Old and Middle stages, is therefore of enormous antiquity; both as a language and in respect of its early literature, its importance in European scholarship is much the same as that of Greek or Sanskrit. Manx, the extinct vernacular of the Isle of Man, and Scottish Gaelic are offshoots of Irish implanted by post-Roman Irish settlements. They became separate languages only during and after the Middle Ages. British, the form of P-Celtic introduced to England, Wales and southern Scotland during the pre-Roman Iron Age, was very closely related to its immediate European parent Gaulish, a language or group of dialects spoken over much of western Europe, including Spain and the north of Italy as well as France. A decent Roman linguist of Caesar's day who understood Gaulish would have been able to follow a conversation in British, and no doubt some did so.

The development of British between 400 BC and AD 400 followed the normal language process, in this case certainly influenced by spoken Latin. The Anglo-Saxon conquests and settlement, sweeping westwards and isolating major regions, hastened the growth of Late British proto-dialects, which gradually became Cumbric in the north and northwest (long extinct), Cornish in the southwest (extinct since the 18th century), and Welsh. In the far north of Scotland there seems to have been an archaic or separate British dialect known as P-Celtic Pictish, of which we know very little. In post-Roman times a substantial emigration from southern Britain, particularly from the southwest, took sufficient Britons across the Channel to Armorica, now Brittany, to implant their own speech, now Breton. Substantially the same as Cornish until Norman times, Breton became a very different tongue with distinctive regional forms under the influence of French. It remains a matter of hot debate to what extent, if any, Breton conceals a much earlier element of surviving Gaulish.

Whether spoken naturally as the home or 'cradle' tongue, used to form place and personal names, or employed (or revived) for cultural and political ends, language is absolutely central to the entire concept of Celticness or Celtdom. It is this, not history or outward physical appearance, that distinguishes a Celt. There is in terms of physical anthropology an extremely general correlation between high incidence of blood group A in eastern and northeast England, and high frequencies of B, AB and O in parts of Wales, Scotland, and western and southwest Ireland; just as true fair hair, popularly believed to point to a Scandinavian background, does happen to be commonest in East Anglia and Lincolnshire. But centuries of internal migration in and between Britain and Ireland make these observations very dubious as any kind of distinction between Celt and Saxon (or Viking), and in any case the blood-group gene frequencies may to an unascertainable extent refer to prehistoric, pre-Celtic, settlement and movement.

2 Llanfairpwll . . ., the Anglesey railway halt with the longest name in the Welsh language – a language directly descended from native British spoken in Roman times.

3 A modern road sign in Celtic
Britain (Cornwall). Only
'Newmill' is immediately
intelligible.

The language history of the British Isles is by far the most revealing
clue to ethnic and political diversity, and is still the principal key to what
most people mean by Celtic Britain. Excluding Brittany and certain small
emigrant communities in the Americas, the present status of Celtic has to
be estimated from the 1981 national British census returns. In Scotland
some 83,000 (1.6 per cent) recorded themselves as Gaelic speakers. Wales
has a much higher proportion, over half a million at 18.9 per cent, and
indeed Welsh, a rich flexible language capable of accommodating modern
notions, is arguably now dividing into distinct literary and colloquial sub-
forms. In both Cornwall and the Isle of Man there are eager bands of
speakers and writers of revived Cornish and Manx, but only in their
hundreds.

The combined total population of Ireland is just under five million.
Modern Irish is constitutionally the first language of the Republic and is
therefore upheld through official use, the support of the Church and the
entire educational system. On the other hand the communities, mostly in
the far west, where Irish has been continuously the vernacular since
prehistory will account only for a small percentage. Probably less than a
fifth of the Irish are fluent in their own language. An Aran fisherman
speaks it naturally; a civil servant from Dublin must learn it, as a would-
be English Eurocrat must learn French or German; the average Dublin
taxi-driver knows only the odd phrase, because his normal speech is a
modified and rather old-fashioned dialect of English. Finally it has to be
said that, very small children and aged Gaels excepted, it is extremely
doubtful that any monoglot British or Irish Celtic-speakers persist.
Celticism implies bilingualism.

Again, it might be possible to imply something of Celtic Britain today not so much by what people believe themselves to be as by the way they vote. The centralization of government in southeast England (London, Reading, Basingstoke, Milton Keynes) and the general belief that unequal distributions of wealth and resources favour that area unduly produce, cyclically, reactions through the ballot box, about the only channel of protest open to the average citizen. Anti-centralism is the regional protest vote, and the anti-central regions are predominantly Celtic in origin. In the October 1974 General Election, 28.5 million votes were cast, nearly 22 million being either for the Labour Party (returned with 40.2 per cent) or the Conservatives. At that time proposals for devolution in home-affairs government for Scotland, with rather slighter concessions for Wales, were much aired. The Scottish Nationalists, and their Welsh counterparts Plaid Cymru ('Party of Wales'), polled over a million votes, 3.5 per cent of the national total. It is probable that among the 5 million and more Liberal voters there were, as traditionally there have long been, about the same number of Celtic regional protesters.

However one seeks to define or to pin down Celtic Britain today, few seem to understand – though perhaps rather more in Britain and elsewhere *should* understand – the connection between the British Isles of the 1980s and the Britannia which the Romans partly absorbed in AD 43 and relinquished untidily four centuries later. This comment leaves aside the history of Ireland, not the least tragic aspect of which is that it has apparently been beyond the comprehension of almost every British politician. Celticness, for better or worse, is still part of the way of life for millions of people. There have, in harsh reality, been only two stages at which Britain itself was predominantly Celtic in most or all senses. One was the pre-Roman Iron Age, following the arrival of bands of Celts from the Continent. The other began early in the 5th century AD and, being curtailed by English or Scandinavian settlement, was of shorter or longer duration according to geography. It was once the fashion to discuss this second phase without any reference to modern times. To do so now might seem like discussing the discovery of America by the Europeans, without explaining why hundreds of millions south of the Panama Canal speak Spanish and Portuguese or why Quebec looks so firmly still to France. The past is always more interesting when it can be connected to the present, and when we can appreciate past events in the light of our own experience. This book prefers to spell out the link at the beginning of the story, not at its end. We are, by definition, looking backwards from the 1980s. The gap in time between the contemporary world and post-Roman Celtic Britain is real and enormous, but even the outline of a proper explanation will help to bridge it.

2·The end of Roman Britain

T
HE ROMANS encountered the British as an agglomeration of farming tribes, in various degrees of sophistication, linked mainly by proximity and a common language. Inter-tribal disputes would have been frequent and the concepts that we associate with early European civilization, if present, were so in a most rudimentary way. Four hundred years later, at which time Roman control persisted mainly on paper, Britain had received the indelible stamp of Mediterranean-centred institutions. If we choose to speculate what 5th-century Britain might have been like had there been no Caesar, no Claudius, no Conquest and no *Britannia*, Ireland during its Early Christian period offers us some guidance; but we do not have to explore this.

The existence of Britain would have been known to European Celts as long as they could make out the White Cliffs of Dover or cross the Channel in fine weather. In the Greek or Roman world such first-hand information was confined to sailors and explorers, whose practical observations and measurements could then be embroidered by learned stay-at-homes – the early Classical geographers and astronomers. The oldest (?4th-century BC) name for Britain was *Albion*, one that has persisted thinly in verse; 'perfidious Albion' (*perfide Albion*) is dubiously attributed to Napoleon Buonaparte. However a later and more widely used name seems to have begun as *Prettania*, and then *Brettania*, becoming fixed as *Britannia* in Latin by Caesar's day. Ireland was first met by the Greeks as *Ierne* (or *Ivernia*, *Ibernia*; *Hibernia* in Latin). This has certainly survived. The contemporary Éire and the poetic 'Erin' come from Old Irish *Ériu*, with its dative and genitive *Érinn*, *Érenn*.

It will assist perspective if we recognize that the Romans were never supermen, nor was Rome – homeland, or expanding empire – in quite the same superior position as 19th-century Europeans in parts of Africa. The whole Italian peninsula had once been just another region of prehistoric Europe with loose agrarian tribes speaking related dialects, jostling with older aboriginals like the Etruscans, and subject to primitive beliefs. *This* region attained the stages of what we are pleased to define as civilization – cities, roads, an agricultural surplus, trading colonies, centralized power, a standing army and systems of law and learning – many centuries before Britain, under the influence of more advanced neighbours to the east and southeast. The Roman conquest of Gaul (covering a larger area than France today) led inexorably to the annexation of Britain with all its natural resources, supposed and real, if only to deny its cross-Channel use as a refuge for disaffected Gauls. The military conquest, hampered by an absence of roads and reliable route-maps and by the presence of very much more woodland and dense scrub than we envisage now, took place with speed and efficiency. The whole history of warfare implies that trained troops, held steady by discipline, regular pay and food and the promise of booty, will subdue much larger numbers of temporarily organized enthusiasts similarly armed (in this case, principally with sword and spear). The Britons may have had their light chariots, but they can have known nothing of overnight defence, siege warfare or the techniques that caused thousands of legionaries to make a single swift tactical move. In any case, the subjugation of Britannia, initially manifested by force of arms, was in reality something other; not the replacement of one national rule by a stronger alternative, but the imposing of an evolved system of government where none had existed.

Early Celtic society possessed a stratification that must have developed during prehistory, can be traced in other areas of the Indo-European world and was the subject of comment by Romans. Caesar was aware that the Gauls were divided between *druides*, priests; *equites*, noble or free warriors; and *plebs*, the common people or unfree agriculturalists. From the warrior caste the Celts chose their kings, the word for which (-*rix*, Irish *ri*) is the same as the Latin *rex* (= reg-s). And like Gaul, the Britain which the Romans annexed was divided among separate peoples or tribes whose names are known from a variety of sources. Some were descriptive: Catuvellauni, 'men good in battle', Atrebates, 'The Inhabitants, The Settlers', Selgovae, 'The Hunters', and Ordovices, 'Hammer-Fighters'. Others may have held the sense of 'Worshippers or followers of the God (named)', like the Dumnonii (of *Dumnonos*) and Parisi.

It would be a mistake to assume that the Romans found England and Wales neatly split into a series of individual kingdoms each with clearly defined boundaries, and having exactly parallel institutions. Archaeology shows us that some of these tribes, like the Dumnonii in southwest Britain and the Brigantes in Yorkshire, represented Iron Age people who had held large tracts for centuries; while in the southeast there were others of relatively recent establishment, having certain contacts still with the Gauls and indeed starting to copy Roman innovations, like issuing their own coinage. We have no real idea precisely how any individual tribe perceived its own territory or kingdom; but since wealth resided in agricultural produce, exclusive rights to land on a family or tribal basis were vital rights, to be maintained and defended.

Warfare, accordingly, would normally have involved the pursuance of these rights or the attainment of dynastic arrangements, on a tribal scale. Only exceptionally should we imagine the collation of anything like a larger army to meet such external threats as the Roman invasion, or Agricola's later Scottish campaign. In peace, the cement of early Celtic society was something that can be called 'clientship', an intricate balance

4 Tombstone of a non-Roman cavalryman (Rufus Sita, of the Sixth Thracian Cohort) spearing a barbarian. From Gloucester, 1st century AD.

of rights and privileges, duties and obligations, set in a pyramid from the ruler down to the least free and most humble tribesmen. The pre-1745 Scottish Highlands clan system was a late but genuine instance. One such duty may have been that of bearing arms. The British *corio-* meant firstly the tribal militia or trained band, those men bound to take up weapons and come together when fighting was required; and secondly, since it enters into Romano-British place-names, 'hosting-place', the traditional rallying points for such bands – hence, too, because of this important function, perhaps even 'tribal centre'. There were Gaulish tribes bearing names like Tricorii and Petrucorii, 'People of the Three (or Four) Hosts'.

The Romans were familiar with the Celtic habit of dividing up the countryside tribally, and they were able to accommodate something of this system in their own organization. Britain (England and Wales) is relatively a small country, but then as now still too large and diverse to be administered as a single entity. It is true that in the 3rd century the Romans did divide Britannia – a civil diocese within the much greater Prefecture of the Gauls – into two provinces: the south of England and Wales as Britannia *Superior*, and the north of England as Britannia *Inferior* ('higher' and 'lower' in the sense of nearer to, and further from, Rome itself). But internally the Roman territorial unit was an admission of a tribal area under the title of *civitas*. Though *civitates* (plur.) are sometimes translated as 'cantons', on the analogies of the Swiss system or the federated German *Lände*, it has always been difficult to pin down a precise definition. Roman political concepts included a philosophy wherein the countryside was subordinate to, and intended as a life-support base for, the all-important urban centres. If this is accepted, a civitas was at once a definite territory with its inhabitants, the principal town ('civitas capital') from which it was controlled, and the abstract concept of an increasingly self-governed community limited to that area for purposes of administration, tax collection and the upholding of commerce and law. This last notion could be expressed as *respublica* (a 'republic', unit of civil administration, or autonomous community) in such inscriptions as *civit(atis) Silurum respublica* and *r(es)p(ublica) c(ivitatis) D(obunnorum)* – the Silures of southeast Wales and Dobunni of the Cotswolds being pre-Roman British tribes. Within a civitas, though we have little direct evidence about this, there could have been subordinate divisions; the *pagus*, a kind of rural district, or *vici*, or rural townships. The identities of British Celtdom were, in some cases, sharpened rather than obliterated. And it is important to note that Rome, employing such tribal identities to form some of the civitates, apparently found it necessary to create new ones (of the Cantiaci in Kent, the Regni or Regini in Sussex and the Belgae in Hampshire and Wiltshire).

One Roman legacy to Britain was thus the provision of a political geography that might otherwise never have come about. Since some of the civitates perpetuated an older territorialism with, presumably,

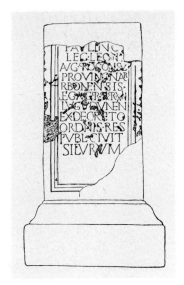

5, 6 **The Roman legacy: civil administration** (*Left*) The eventual 4th-century division of Roman Britain into provinces (actual boundaries conjectural), with the locations and modern names of the provincial capitals. (*Right*) Inscription from Caerwent, shortly before AD 220, set up by the decree of the council of *Respublica Civitatis Silurum*, the government of the canton of the Silures.

uneven land-ownership tribally sanctioned, and since Rome possessed (over and above the almost universal extension of her citizenship to free peoples within the empire during the 2nd century) a stratified hierarchical society, British families were thus able to continue a system of social grade by descent and the unequal distribution of wealth and property. Native concepts of nobility, even possibly of some kind of ancestral local royalty in abeyance, and of the right to command could be transmuted into Roman civil office. Each civitas had an *ordo*, not unlike a modern British County Council. An inscribed early 3rd-century pedestal at Caerwent, honouring T. Claudius Paulinus shortly before he became the governor of Britannia Inferior, was erected *ex decreto ordinis* (*respublica civitatis Silurum*) – 'By Order of the Council'. A national structure of this kind needed a constant supply of local gentry obliged to serve on their ordines, and as magistri and decuriones. It can be concluded that on the whole the system worked. The Roman aim was to delegate, as soon as practicable, the burdens of local government, the administration of law and tax collection to their imperial recruits. It would never have been possible to staff and to carry out all this machinery of rule from the centre.

The Romanization of Celtic Britain could be presented in many forms. For our purposes, as we move later to the Britain of post-Roman times, the most revealing side is that exemplified by the whole political restructuring – an unwitting gift of *shape* and *order* that may help to explain later events; and with it, the advent of Latin, not just a spoken language linking Britannia with the rest of Europe and the Mediterranean, but the very basis of *writing* and therefore of learning, culture, command and the transmission of ideas.

The gift of form may also have touched, profoundly, the messy and sprawling world of pre-Christian religion. The Celts had their priesthood, known to the Romans as *druides*, operating locally if in some fashion linked nationally. Our knowledge of it comes from Classical allusions to Celtic religious practices (with the fair assumption that, here, Britain resembled Gaul); from divine names occurring in inscriptions and place-names; and from reconstructions drawn cautiously from the oldest strata of Irish and Welsh heroic literature and verse.

There were pagan deities on a large scale. A Celtic European war-god Camulos was commemorated in Camulodunum (Colchester: 'C's Fort') and Camulosessa (some fort in Scotland: 'C's Seat') as well as in some Continental place-names. It was the Roman custom to promote identifications (*interpretationes*) between divine beings of their own pantheon and those of peoples whom they absorbed. Typically, a sacrificial altar from Bar Hill, Dunbarton, bears an inscription to DEO MAR[TI] CAMULO, 'The God Mars-Camulos'. Similarly Maponus, a British 'Divine Youth' figure, is known as Apollo Maponus; and Sulis, a mysterious goddess presiding over the hot springs at Bath, was worshipped as Sulis Minerva.

The foundations of the Romans' own paganism, Emperor-worship aside, must once have been very similar to those of the Celts. The Roman catalogue included deities deemed responsible for distinct aspects of life and affairs, but there were others once linked to specific tribes and locations and still others who had personified rivers, wells, forests or the chase. The retention of certain animals and birds as attributes points to a much earlier level of belief, one partly maintained in a background of private sprites and godlings, the Roman *lares familiares* (like the 'Brownies' of medieval England). The Celts had not yet acquired appropriate settings for representations of gods, something unlikely in the absence of town life. Insofar as there were Celtic temples at all, these were either sites of prehistoric character related to mortuary enclosures, ritual pits or constructions imitative of ordinary dwellings; or else natural spots sacred in themselves. Groves or wooded areas were favoured. The British and Gaulish *nemet-on*, 'sacred grove', is seen in *Nemeto statio*, a Roman fort somewhere in Devon, and again in the name of the spa at Buxton (*Aquae Arnemetiae*), 'Waters of the (goddess) Arnemetia' (She-who-stands-before-the-sacred-grove).

To this pervasive sphere of existence the Romans may well have brought more than might appear, and something relevant to later centuries. Sculpture in the round (developed far away, among the fine

7, 8 **The Roman legacy: religion** (*Above*) Identification of Roman with native deities – an altar to Apollo Maponus from Corbridge on Hadrian's Wall. (*Right*) Romano-Celtic realizations of deities – a small bronze mount, 13 cm high, of Minerva in animal headdress and corselet with Medusa head, her foot on her sacred Little Owl. Market Lavington, Wiltshire.

limestone marbles alien to Britannia), bronze statuettes, inscribed tablets and sacrificial altars now led to the depiction of native deities and the recital of their names. Even in remote corners of Britain, efforts could be made with intractable local stones. In pre-Roman days the average Briton was aware of the gods only as amorphous and dangerous forces, perhaps possessing gender and names but not otherwise defined. They required at all times to be placated through sacrifice and ritual, or propitiated lest frightful evils should befall. At a tribal level certain rivers (*Deva*, the Chester Dee and others; *Brigantia*, the Brent; probably *Sabrina*, the Severn) seem to have been personified as goddesses. Religious phenomenology suggests they would have been seasonal consorts for tribal kings. Some obscure northern peoples bore names hinting at almost totemic divine animals – the Epidii, Bibroci and Orci, names with the Celtic words for horse, beaver and boar.

Under the stimuli of Greek thought and the growth of their own complex political and commercial world, the Romans had arrived at a very different relationship with their gods. They managed to bring them into the sphere of everyday living. These beings, entrusted with the prosperity of Rome and with clear departments of life and death, were supra-humans in the sky, but ones condescending to take part in a construct of *balance*. In this, men ceased merely to ward off shapeless ills and were permitted to approach the gods, as they would their business associates, with requests, bargains and promises. The little votive altars that dotted Roman Britain and all other provinces by the thousands record, publicly, the fulfilment of vows. Honour is paid, libations poured and sacrifices offered as a thanks for favours and relief. The Celtic deities of Britain, in their own or in Roman shape, partook fully. Roman temples, providing visible (often impressive) foci for worship and for communal ceremonies, anchored the major native deities in the Romanized townscape and countryside – even if private *sacra* persisted amid the outlying forests, with their springs and crags. The whole process, as Professor John Mann has pointed out, may for the first time have brought about the actual creation of Celtic deities as individual personalities. The stage was being set for the introduction of a much more pervasive and advanced national faith, one also requiring temples, a correct balance with the unseen, and a personified deity: Christianity.

As for language, the prime distinction between British and Latin lay in the odd fact that the former was not, on the whole, ever written. In France and surrounding regions, Gaulish was replaced as an everyday speech by Latin, and by the 5th century was a rustic and faintly comic curiosity. The parallel British language, by contrast, was never lost. There seems however to have been an almost total block against using Latin letters to convey anything save simple British names. Why this obstacle existed is the subject of much discussion. The steady reconstruction of British, an impressive and convincing achievement, has

9 The Cucullati or Hooded Ones: a mysterious trio of deities, relief from Housesteads on Hadrian's Wall.

been won from comparative linguistic studies, not from any body of narrative inscriptions or parallel texts. Its structure, with familiar cases and declensions and verb endings, was not unlike that of Latin. Theoretically if the Latin ABC could be used to write out *cervus rufus*, 'red stag', it could just as well have expressed the British equivalent (*coccos carvos*). The explanation may be largely psychological. Latin – the tongue of government, the army and the dominant power – was regarded as integral with the writing system that accompanied it. British had no such counterpart, and failed to develop it before a later period of its daughter-languages.

Very few Celtic words were borrowed into Latin, and then mostly in Gaul before the conquest of Britain (a few, like *alouette* and *bijou*, survive in French). British and Irish became studded with Latin borrowings. Some were words for objects and notions previously unknown, like *fenestra*, 'window', *brassica*, 'cabbage', and *mercatus*, 'market' – now

29

Welsh *ffynster*, *bresych(en)*, Cornish *marchas* and Breton *marchad*. Others show supersession of a British device by a superior Roman counterpart as when Latin *pons*, *pontem*, 'constructed bridge', Welsh and Cornish *pont*, ousted British *briva*, probably 'plank (over a stream)'. If we had lost all the direct evidence of history and the powerful inferential aids of archaeology, a reconstruction of the impact of Rome could be made from the scale and nature of these borrowings on their own.

Celts customarily possessed a one-word name. This could be a simple and traditional one, or more impressive in the case of persons of rank. The Gaulish king Vercingetorix's name implies something like 'King-who-tramples-upon (his enemies)'. The formal Roman name-system was multiple; a personal or familiar name, but with others indicating parentage, the old Roman citizen voting tribes, geographical origin and, in the case of incorporated peoples, Imperial or prominent names relating to the date at which freedom or citizenship was conferred. This led to hybrids. We have Tiberius Claudius *Cogidubnus* (an early and amenable British kinglet), and Gaius *Verecundius* Severus. Single names, Celtic or Roman, did continue among the lower orders, the British names assuming written Latin forms like Cintusmus, Vallaunius, Cunomolius, Belismicus and Senovara. Eventually many Roman names found their way into British and later languages. Is it always spotted today that little Welsh boys called Tegid and Iestyn perpetuate the names Tacitus and Justinus as walking symbols of their nation's interesting past?

For the face of Britain by far and away the most striking imposition – one destined to outlive Roman government – lay in what can be summed up as *planning*. The native British were in the main farmers. Differing emphases on arable for cereal production, pasture for stock, or a mixed farming mode can be explained by variable geography (e.g., soil qualities) and ancestral habits. We do not know precisely how land-holdings were owned, save that any tenure would have been customary at best. One early view of Britannia – Julius Caesar's, from Gaul – was of a densely populated land rich in timber and minerals, with a mild climate; predominantly arable in the southeast, but otherwise given over to cattle. In 54 BC Caesar found it possible to extract a very large tribute of grain from the Trinovantes – they covered Suffolk and Essex, still a part of Britain's corn belt. This roseate picture of the British potential awaiting Roman hands is later repeated by Gildas after 500 ('excellent for vigorous agriculture, and mountains especially suited to varying pasture for animals') and by Bede in 731 ('rich in grain crops and timber, and in pastures for stock and draught-animals; furthermore, vines are grown in some places'). It was an attraction that the Romans did not overlook. Here was a country able to feed the necessary garrisons and to support, through proper distribution, the likely towns. The technological level of British agriculture was, notably in the south, much the same as in pre-Roman Gaul. Centuries of Roman ways were to raise that level. One

10, 11 **The Roman legacy: building** (*Above*) The evolved Celtic tradition of the circular farmhouse – the 1976 reconstruction at Butser Hill, Dorset, 12.8 m across. (*Below*) The Roman rectilinear tradition – villa with farm outbuildings at Llantwit Major, Glamorgan, south Wales.

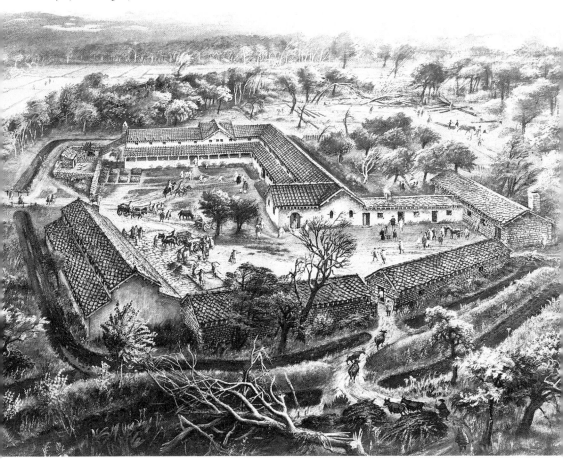

marked change was the growth of a whole range of farm-buildings – barns, byres, granaries, sheds and other stores – similar to those of medieval England.

But to this broad agrarian canvas, so agreeably fresh and simple, Roman power added a system of proper roads. Military and official in origin and upkeep, they formed the spines for innumerable systems of lanes and minor ways, swallowing up the tracks of prehistory. The paved route broad enough for a marching column with its baggage train, or for

12, 13 **The Roman legacy: roads and fortifications** (*Left*) The 1¼-mile stretch of Roman road excavated and preserved at foundation level on Wheeldale Moor, Yorkshire. (*Above*) Roman shore-fort walling at Burgh Castle, Suffolk.

the easement of wheeled traffic, and the very concept of measured distances (with milestones proclaiming Imperial titles and the device of writing) made an impressive network. It was redolent of authority and progress. Towns, with their craft shops, their market-places and squares, temples and public buildings, were equally remarkable to Celts who, alone, had not progressed further than something like a large Zulu kraal expressed in timberwork. Most of the terms for masonry and building had to be taken from Latin – right through to *maceria* ('a masonry wall'), giving Welsh *magwyr* and Cornish *magor* in one early place-name sense of 'building-remains', 'ancient ruins'.

It is well nigh impossible today to think ourselves back into the position of a Roman Briton in the 4th century. Britannia *was* a part of the greater Rome. The rough existed with the smooth: high infant mortality, taxation, inflation and recurrent threats of internal and external disturbance, alongside the general stability of Romanitas and the steady material improvements. But the civilized regions still adjoined (for those who happened to think about it) a reservoir of Celtic barbarism north of the Antonine Wall, westward across the Irish Sea and rather less alarmingly so in the mountains of Wales. If in 1900 the British had abruptly quitted all India, a Bombay businessman might similarly have pondered, uneasily, about the so-called martial races of the north, and the wild Afridis and Pathans beyond them. Huge old India – with its railways, Grand Trunk Roads and innumerable barrack-towns – did at least ensure considerable distances between its Europeanized cities and the frontier savagery. Britannia, so much smaller, had in addition a lengthy and generally open coastline; it could be attacked by sea, and not only by Continental enemies.

The steady collapse of Roman rule and order during the later 4th century AD is amply documented in standard works and need not be set out in any detail here. Internal troubles, to be clarified through socio-economic analysis rather than by archaeological results, mirrored locally a wider Imperial malaise. The population had undoubtedly grown, mostly during the 3rd and 4th centuries and in a phase of favourable climate, relative freedom from epidemic disease and relative improvements in public health. A peak (for England and Wales) of between three and four millions is now not just a guess but an informed estimate.

Such population increases, and the whole economic framework, implied a certain vulnerability to any breakdown in urban life, food supplies and dependence upon those ordered ways protected by the army. Tribes from the north – mainly Picts, reported as arriving by sea as well as across the defended land frontier – posed the greatest danger when their incursions were matched by others from Ireland, and by the attacks of ferocious Saxons, non-Celtic barbarians who dwelt beyond the limits of Roman Gaul and the Rhineland provinces. Late Roman coastal defences in Britain like the shore forts, with improvements to the naval capacity, indicate the response. It was not sufficient to prevent an invasion from all three sources in 367, one remembered as the Barbarian Conspiracy. There were periods of respite, but broken by further similar events. The effect of purely Roman power-games, as when in 383 Magnus Maximus withdrew much of the field army to support his Gaulish venture, was to oblige the Britons – weakened by the loss of professional garrisons – to look to their own defence.

The stories of post-Roman Cornwall, Scotland and Wales are resumed in separate chapters. That of Ireland is not and can be summed up here. Ireland, Hibernia, was the country that Rome omitted to conquer. Tacitus, in his memoir (AD 97–98) of his father-in-law Gnaeus Julius Agricola, implies that the Romans believed Ireland to be a fruitful land, one that would be easy in the picking. Since they also believed it to lie approximately between Britain and Spain, its acquisition would most suitably have rounded off the westernmost advance of empire. Tacitus attributes to Agricola the comment that, if the British were to be completely subdued, it would be a good idea to extinguish by arms any such adjoining freehold of non-Roman liberty.

The point is that Ireland *was* known, in very vague terms from the early geographers, and now in a different way because (according to Tacitus) merchants – British or Gaulish – traded through its eastern and southern harbours. During the Roman centuries Irish-British relationships were intricate, and it is inaccurate still to portray them solely in terms of Irish raiders and pirates. There is good evidence that Romano-British traders reached not just the coastal havens but points well inland, via the larger navigable rivers like the Barrow. They would have set up entrepots, and possibly encouraged reciprocal Irish ventures to western Britain. Latin loan-words in Irish, it is argued, were acquired over a period of centuries. The earliest group, antedating the main body of Christian Latin terminology associated with Patrick and further Christian contacts from the 5th century, seems to be concerned with the vocabulary of Roman commerce, literature, money, arms and material equipment.

It is quite difficult to estimate the late Roman population of Ireland, because most of the indicators so used in the case of Roman Britain are missing. If the picture now emerging from field survey and archaeological research offers proper guidance, we can guess that the Irish underwent some such parallel growth. The social structure and settlement pattern, a nearly complete checkerboard of tiny kingdoms subject to periodic groupings, would have encouraged the emigration of any surplus numbers partly because of the growing demands on good-quality pasture and grazing that arose in a country where stockbreeding was a major activity. From the 4th century AD, if not slightly earlier, the Irish began to form new settlements in parts of Wales, with western Scotland, the Isle of Man and southwest Britain as areas of secondary colonization. These are to be seen, not as nests of wintering pirates, but as genuine agricultural settlements. The main differences between these Irish colonists and their British hosts lay in custom and language. Their everyday lives and simple material cultures were far less distinguishable. In Ireland, quite apart from any British bands engaged in trade, there were numerous Britons who had been captured to serve as unfree labourers; enslavement of their own defeated enemies was an Irish practice.

Eventually, as we know, certain of the Irish colonies in Britain which had initially retained their own languages and leaders were simply absorbed by the indigenous Celtic populace. That in the Isle of Man was later to experience Scandinavian overlordship, but nevertheless managed to produce the Manx language. In the west of Scotland the Irish gave the country its Gaelic language and eventually its very name. The Scots (*Scoti*, *Scotti*), wherever settled, were originally the natives of *Scotia*, a general term for Ireland that from late Roman times replaced the older Hibernia. Britain's cultural debt to the Irish, something that began centuries earlier than W. B. Yeats and George Bernard Shaw, will be mentioned again. Ireland, if far enough from Britain to be a separate country, stands none the less too close to have experienced a completely separate history.

It is exceptionally difficult to try to sum up, for the end of the 4th century AD, the extent and nature of Britain's other and greater debt to Rome; in certain respects it becomes far more apparent in later centuries. Similarly, the retention of so much inherited and preserved from pre-Roman Celtic Britain is apparent – when not obscured or obliterated by the English settlements – mainly from the later 5th century, after the dust of AD 400 to 450 has settled. It then becomes a matter of distinguishing between revival and continuity. The latter is betrayed by Christianity, literacy and Latinity, and the diminished sense of participation in a changed empire; certainly not by any maintenance of towns, communications and the unsteady late Roman economy. The former is the inevitable re-statement of Celticness – to be detected in language, in institutions and at a detailed regional level in certain kinds of art. The crucial phase was the 5th century AD. If British prehistory ended with the conquest of AD 43, the 5th century is still historically the most obscure, if still also the most intensively studied, and even a bald summary of current thought must occupy the next chapter.

3·Celtic Britain:the 5th and 6th Centuries

THE STORY OF BRITAIN from shortly after 400 to 597, when the arrival of a Papal mission in Kent anchors the history of the *English* (if not of the British) to European sequences, can all too easily resemble a Will-of-the-wisp. Today's reader, venturing beyond popular accounts into textbooks and even into certain specialized journals, may well slam them all down in despair – as a prime instance of Now you see it, now you don't. We are not short of names, events, localities and supposedly firm dates proper to these centuries; the difficulty is that with appallingly few exceptions we are still uncertain what they mean, or how we are to make interpretations corresponding to past reality.

The sources are generally thought of as two-fold. There are historical notices relating to Britain, mostly comment from afar on the manner in which Britannia was lost to Rome; and there are the inferences and demonstrations (as to historical probabilities) arising from archaeological research, particularly when expressed as distribution maps. The two classes do not inevitably agree. One can add a third source – a 'linguistic archaeology' of conclusions taken from the study of languages and place-names. These permit statements about the interplay of spoken (Vulgar) Latin, spoken Late British and spoken Primitive Anglo-Saxon, thus giving rise to new ideas about the relations between the users of these tongues.

At the moment, a minimal view of the period must be sought, in the hope of avoiding confusion and of providing a broadly acceptable account. Two major strands can be teased out of the overall tangle, and the story of British Christianity (resumed in Chapter 7) may eventually rank as a third. Our standpoint will be that of present-day England, touching only slightly on Wales and for the moment ignoring most of Scotland. Since, temporally, most matters have to be approached in the light of a descent, regression or dissolution from the last hundred years of Roman Britannia, this earlier portion of Britain's history between 400 and 800 can – loosely, but justifiably – be labelled *sub-Roman*.

The collapse during the 5th century

First, then, if it is contended that the principal Roman contribution had been the imposition of order in a hundred different modes (political, technological, social, linguistic and religious being merely the most obvious), the general course of affairs in the 5th century demonstrates that the structure of Britannia, left to itself, was inadequate to uphold the imprint of Rome – to survive in isolation, maintaining the fruits of progress and discipline. Rome had, after all, not managed to conquer the entire Old World. Where the limits of her empire adjoined the territories of non-Roman free peoples capable of bearing arms, and of casting their eyes on superior resources known to them through trade or individual military service, a steady state could be maintained only by frontier defences and garrisons. In Britain, as elsewhere, there came a point where these defences were now too nominal, the garrisons too deeply committed to auxiliary troops, federates and native militias, for the deterrence of invaders (many of whose ancestors had at some time past been ready to engage actual Roman legions). The run-down of full Roman military cover, the non-replacement of senior Roman figures as national and provincial governors and the absence of any effective means (beyond the tiny scale of local communities) to enforce law and order were, in Britannia's case, coincident with factors of a different sort – for instance, economic difficulties. Inflation, a real shortage of low denomination coinage and a breakdown in systems of marketing the farm and workshop products led towards an invitation to lawlessness.

We shall probably continue to be unsure to what precise extent the technology of late Roman Britain (other than agriculture) was in either native or non-native hands. Quarrying and simple alluvial mining suggest British contractors and native labour; dockside trading and warehousing do not. Given the ethnic make-up of the late empire the point may not be very material; but the maintenance of roads and waterways, town defences and sewers, aqueducts and most public-utility buildings like markets, temples, courts and barracks would always have involved much labour under skilled direction. Without regular support in the shape of food and housing, let alone valid pay, no public workforce can be kept at its task.

In short, if one can make no more than informed guesses at the manner in which Britannia reverted to sub-Roman Celtic Britain, history and archaeology combine to inform us that this did happen. It may have happened relatively swiftly. If the last bastion of Roman life and ways can, vaguely, be seen in southern and southeast England, this may be only because those parts had been earliest and most intensively transformed into something resembling a province nearer the Imperial heartland. As to the simple question of which parties might be expected to have grabbed power when Roman control was withdrawn, there is a simple answer: those in a position to do so – either through possessing an armed following, or through the ability to persuade enough people that their state of command descended from some earlier Roman office and was thereby, in Roman or sub-Roman terms, legitimized.

14 Bronze objects from a military burial, probably of a Germanic federate settler, from the end of Roman Britain. Grave I, Dyke Hills, Dorchester-on-Thames, Oxfordshire.

The English conquest

The second strand involves the most successful of external threats, that of the Saxons. The German-speaking peoples whose homelands lay in a free Europe north of the Rhine and Danube, up into Scandinavia and the western Baltic, had by the first half of the 5th century changed the face of the Roman empire. Any atlas will show permanent reminders of this. The mighty Goths penetrated on the one hand into Russia, on the other into Aquitaine, Italy and sacred Rome itself. The Vandals marched through Spain (whence Andalusia) and across the Straits of Gibraltar to found a small kingdom in north Africa. Franks, Langobardi, Alemanni and Burgundians moved into much of the western empire; Burgundy, and the Italian Lombardy, commemorate this, as does the linguistic division of present Switzerland.

In Roman Britain, various German-speaking groups were already no strangers. Quite apart from 4th-century coastal raids by the wild Saxones (who may in precise ethnic terms have equally been Frisones, Frisians from the low coasts and islands of the Netherlands and the German littoral), numerous such Germans served in the Roman army as individuals, in what amounted to tribal recruitments, and even as noted generals who could aspire to the purple. Veterans settled in Britannia, forming their own language-communities and creating their own burial-grounds (archaeologically detectable through specific pottery and minor metalwork). In the troubled times between 350 and 420-odd, more than one Roman town found, among the rumbustious Anglo-Saxons dwelling outside (and increasingly inside) the city limits, an obvious way to recruit town guards and armed watchmen. The Roman British lumped them together generally as *Saxones* – still the Welsh word *Saeson*, 'English'. The Germanic settlers, earlier on the Continent, similarly possessed a blanket term (*Walhōz*) for all non-German neighbours, Celts pure or Romanized; later, within Britain, this became *Walas*, 'strangers: British'

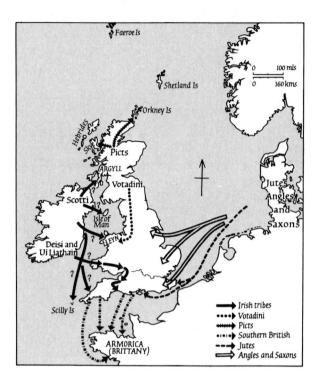

15 Tribal migrations leading to the dismemberment of Roman Britain.

– whence the English people's name for Wales. Though there was no question of direct mutual intelligibility across a divide subsequently sharpened as between Christians and heathens, among those words and terms borrowed into Old English were some from the spoken Latin of Britannia (before and after 400) as well as British ones.

The climax in this relationship might, at the risk of considerable simplification, be seen as arising – inevitably – between irreconcilable interests. Some at least of the British will have wished to preserve the independence, with the material enjoyments most markedly found in ruling circles, of a land now bereft of overt Roman protection. The Anglo-Saxons had through a variety of ways come to know this once rich, agriculturally still desirable, part of the empire; it is abundantly clear that their overwhelming interest lay in the countryside, often well farmed and an arena ripe for expanding settlement, and hardly ever in the alien and unmanageable remains of towns.

On the Continent, the empire was subjected to major barbarian invasions in 407 – disasters at first culminating in the Gothic king Alaric's sack of Rome (410). Military circles in Britannia, now politically as well as geographically distant from Rome, elected a rapid succession of their own pretenders, usurping junior Emperors. In 407 Constantine III may have weakened his British base by taking troops across to Gaul, where he was opposed both by barbarians and by Roman forces loyal to the senior

Emperor or Augustus, Honorius. By 409 Constantine – whom Honorius was obliged to recognize as fellow-Augustus and joint consul for that year – momentarily controlled the prefecture of Gaul and therefore the diocese of Britannia within it.

But Constantine, on a brief campaign in Italy and then in the new prefecture capital at Arles (where he was defeated and slain in 411), could do nothing to protect Britain itself. During 408 there had been a large-scale invasion by barbarians from beyond the Rhine, who must have been Saxons, probably accompanied by Angles from southern Denmark. The British civitates – here this implies the large urban centres, many demonstrably still functioning as such – managed to defend themselves and during 409 to quell if not to expunge this invasion. This is now generally accepted, even if it is unclear how it was accomplished. In 410 however – a year frequently hauled out of the confusion to mark the actual 'end' of Roman Britain – a second crisis caused Honorius to write to the cities of Britain, ordering them once more to look unaided to their own defences. The assumption is that he was responding to their request for a return of the legions, a renewal of military aid.

The interpretations placed on this today include the idea that, parallel to a popular uprising of the oppressed classes in Armorica (Brittany) during 409, there had been a revolt of peasants and slaves in parts of Britain. The cry for aid came, not as a national plea in the face of Saxon enemies, but from those British who were besieged in their hungry towns and who still claimed alone to uphold and to represent Roman legitimacy. If true, a long straggle of unstructured civil war – the have-nots against the haves – characterized the next half-century. We may be in no position to define these troubles, as aspects of sub-Roman British affairs, in the closer light of class, regional, legitimist or dynastic conflicts; but something on these lines did take place. The impact was long remembered. In the 6th century Gildas was able to record that, if by his own day the external wars had ceased, then *bella civilia* – civil fightings – had not. Wrongly or rightly he can be read as implying a sequence of these, from the early 5th century onwards.

Their effect was to speed the dismemberment of Britannia. At first, this may have been into ghost-remnants of the 4th-century provinces and of those civitates which – by virtue of surviving urban capitals – retained any vestiges of the old administrative divisions. The rise of successor native kingdoms was hastened. But central to whatever pattern emerged was still the principal external threat, that of English settlement on a scale too large to dislodge.

The Adventus Saxonum, this nominal, ultimate, single 'Arrival of the Saxons', cannot be given any precision in time through archaeology, even though the diffusion of settlements following some such major conquest is slowly defined from archaeological discoveries and place-name analysis. A single external source, that of the anonymous southern

Gaulish chronicler ascribed to 452, does note that in a year to be equated with AD 441–42 the British provinces, having suffered various disasters and misfortunes, *in dicionem Saxonem rediguntur*; they were 'reduced to Saxon rule'. No subsequent estimations of a date – and this includes Bede's calculations (which favoured a bracket of 446 to 455) – should be allowed to supplant whatever weight attaches to this older notice.

The arrogant usurper

The context for the Adventus, on the other hand, is drawn from British sources, the 6th-century writings of Gildas being the earliest. The event is depicted in terms of cause and effect and, given the tenor of Gildas's *De Excidio Britonum* ('The Ruin of the Britons'), also in terms of Divine retribution visited upon a sinful race.

Gildas's own life and work can be dated only with much uncertainty. He was probably committing his views to writing around the middle of the century in a place and under circumstances where, as he seems to admit, any detailed knowledge of 5th-century British affairs had been lost. The happenings of a hundred or more years beforehand had thus been transmitted mostly by rumour and oral tradition and inevitably were taking on legendary accretions.

He tells us that it had been supposed the Picts and their allied *grassatores Hiberni*, 'the scoundrel Irish', were once more poised to attack sinful Britain, plunged as it was in hatred, quarrels and greed. Failing to mend their ways, the British were next struck by a plague (epidemics are indeed known for early medieval times, but this one lacks secure identification). Alarmed, the British ruling circles called a council. Under the leadership of an 'arrogant usurper' (*superbus tyrannus* – presumably one devoid of a legitimate, Roman-derived, position of national dominance), it was decided to repel the Pictish-Irish invasions from the north by inviting Saxons to defend the land. Three shiploads, duly summonsed, arrived in the east of Britain, as Gildas says, 'ostensibly to fight for our country; in fact to fight *against* it'. On their heels came a much larger Saxon contingent. For a time, these awkward mercenaries were bought off with supplies but, using the pretext of asking for more than could be provided, they rebelled against their hosts and ravaged Britannia – 'all the major towns were laid low'.

It is not known whether the original copy, or the near-contemporary copies, of Gildas's own manuscript named this *superbus tyrannus*. We presume that one of them did so because Bede, who drew on this source (in 725 and 731), knew him as Vertigernus or Uuertigernus. This represents a British name Wortigernos; but note that it is a proper if bombastic personal name (meaning literally 'Over-lord'; a partial analogy is seen in later English royal personal names like Eadbald, 'Happily-Courageous', or Athelstan, 'Noble-Stone, Royal-Jewel'). It is neither the man's title, nor does *superbus tyrannus* translate it. As Vortigern, he passed into legend and the early history of Celtic Britain – the archetypal national mistake-maker, if not betrayer.

The episode may conceal a real, unitary, happening, but its legendary overtones are suspected even at the period of Gildas. One version of the Anglo-Saxon Chronicle, the subsequent compilation that holds the English view of early Britain, portrays the original three boat-loads divided between three German peoples – Saxons, Angles and Jutes – and led by Hengist and Horsa, heroic great-great-grandsons of the god Woden, the Germanic Jupiter figure. More credible, simply because they fell closer in time to Gildas's life, are the circumstances he next relates. A British resistance to the Saxon revolt emerged. It was led by Ambrosius Aurelianus, a man whose family had been honourably prominent in the last decades of Roman Britain, and Gildas states that this man's grandchildren were then living. Eventually, stability was restored through a spectacular British victory, the battle (or siege; we presume a crushing British repulse of Saxon besiegers) known as Mount Badon, *Mons Badonicus*; as Gildas writes, 'more or less the most recent, and not the least notable, of the defeats of the (Saxon) scoundrels'. There followed a kind of peace in his time; though it was not a British recovery of Britannia. Archaeologically, 6th-century conditions can be simplified to a map symbolizing (mostly from archaeology and place-name study) a division of the country with a wavering frontier-belt. Gildas seems to say that there were areas of Britain where, by the 6th century, Britons could not go, and the historian may sooner interpret this as 'a fluid and piecemeal division of land between Briton and barbarian'.

16 A claimed forbear of the 5th-century Aureliani? Dedication slab from Birdoswald, between AD 297 and 305, naming – fourth line down – 'His Perfection Aurelius Arpagus', Praeses or Governor of Roman Britain.

Problems of time and place

These allusions give us no exact dates. If Vortigern's life included episodes datable to 441–42 or 446–55, it would portray a native usurper in the mid-5th century, contemporary with a society producing a legitimist British leader, Ambrosius Aurelianus, whose name was wholly Roman. 'Aurelius' and 'Aurelianus' occur in late Romano-British inscriptions. At this period the baptismal name Ambrosius was probably inspired by that of St Ambrose of Milan, who died in 397. The battle of Mount Badon may have taken place within a decade or so either side of AD 500. Gildas tells us, if we understand him correctly, that he was born in the year of that battle and writes 44 years afterwards – that is, in a period centred on 550.

17–19 **The age of Arthur**
(*Above*) Liddington Castle: an
Iron Age hillfort on a spur of the
chalk downland, south of
Swindon, Wiltshire – is this
Mount Badon? (*Right*) South
Cadbury Castle, near Wincanton,
by the Wiltshire–Somerset
border; an impressive hill, re-
fortified around AD 500 and
identified in local belief as the
Arthurian Camelot since the 16th
century. (*Opposite*) The natural
crag of Bamburgh Castle,
Northumberland, traditional first
fortress of the invading Angles.

Gildas also omits place-names. British resistance to the English may have been centred in southern England or the Midlands (as an area with former civitas capitals). 'Mount Badon' has been sought in many spots, including most fortified hills whose names contain the syllable *Bad-*. Two hillforts in particular, Liddington Castle near Swindon (Wiltshire) and Badbury Rings near Wimborne (Dorset), are the least unlikely. About 35 miles west of these forts is the massive native earthwork-citadel of South Cadbury Castle near Wincanton in Somerset. This, identified in local belief as the Arthurian Camelot since the 16th century, was partly re-fortified and notably re-occupied by persons of importance around 500, as excavated material demonstrates.

It is in this second phase of a British response, leading up to Mount Badon, that later native tradition seems to have picked out a hero-figure, Arthur; not originally a king (*rex*), but in the Roman mould of *dux* (war-leader, field-general). If Gildas singularly fails either to name him or even to imply his existence, the tales of some such hero with his Twelve Great Battles percolated during the following centuries throughout Celtic Britain, from the south of Scotland, down through Cumbria and Wales, and into all of the southwest. It was the elaboration of Arthur's prowess, symbol of the continuity of Britannia against a growing England, and not the recital of Vortigern's betrayal, that held the field. Eventually it passed through the hands of Anglo-Norman embroiderers into the literary stock of medieval Europe, and back into English literature to receive its finest treatment from Alfred, Lord Tennyson.

It becomes depressingly more clear, as analysis proceeds, that Gildas knew (or had decided to say) surprisingly little about events in Britain between 400 and Mount Badon. It is possible that the Saxon *adventus* took place wholly in what is now the north of England; and that Gildas's three ships of Saxons were, as a manifestation of folk tradition, only to be matched by, not identified with, the Hengist-and-Horsa arrival that the English themselves very firmly located at Ebbesfleet in Kent. Naturally we could suppose that, writing from some 6th-century church establishment (Chester has been proposed here), Gildas knew comparatively little of his own Britain at first-hand. He was, as he claims, unable to draw on sequential written accounts, since these had ceased to exist after the early 400s. The kinds of persons likely to have spared any time in recording such matters had long since fled overseas.

There is room to suggest that the pre-Badon half-century of Saxon wars took place in quite a small area, such as the south-central English scenario already implied, and involved only limited military forces. The main damage would have been sporadic attacks by some Saxons or some British. If so, other areas far to the north and west may have retained a degree of sub-Roman ways until late in the 5th century. In Northumbria – the whole northeast of Britain, from southeast Scotland down to Yorkshire – there is a suspicion that relations between incomers and natives were more complex. The predominantly Anglian, not Saxon, settlement of coastal Northumbria led gradually by the later 6th and 7th centuries to Anglian dynasties, ostensibly on the pattern of earlier British rule. It is not clear that this was ever brought about by an overwhelming numerical weight of Angles. In this region of hills and moors and sparsely-settled valleys, sheep country with upland hamlets once one goes inland from the coastal belt, Angles and Britons may have co-existed under Anglian lords and kings.

Early British kings and kingdoms

Gildas's further references to kings, public office-holders, private notables, bishops, priests and judges are proper only to his own century. He fails to say much about any corresponding principalities and native states, institutions whose geo-political existence would in any case have been irrelevant to his main theme. The rise of the individual Anglo-Saxon kingdoms can be sketched from the writings of Bede (a first-hand authority for the late 7th and early 8th centuries), from lesser and near-contemporary Northumbrian writings, and from chronicles, charters, and limited ecclesiastical records. On the other hand, we do not have comparable or sufficient material to do the same for the sub-Roman British kingdoms.

Major problems include the extent to which, if at all, their shapes were influenced by the older Roman divisions of Britannia; details of their locations, or what constituted boundaries between them; and lastly, except from very general analogy (which rests, rather insecurely, mainly on the early social history of un-Romanized Ireland), precisely what ideas were involved in the contemporary British notion of 'a kingdom'. That kingdoms existed is agreed. What is so difficult to detect is the pre-450, or pre-500, process that involved their formation.

The post-Roman era saw a growing consciousness by the native British population – one sharpened by the divisions between themselves and the English, differing as they did in speech and ethnic origin and to some extent religion – that the land was or had been their own. Though after 400 a few Britons chose to think of themselves still as *Romani*, Roman citizens, their descendants preferred to be (in Latin) *Britanni, Brittoni, Brettones*, etc. Those who migrated across the Channel to the Armorican region of northwest Gaul gave 'Brittany' its very name. The British also possessed a second generic name in their own tongue, *Com-brogi* – '(those) with (the same) border; co-countrymen'. Its universal currency is seen through its base for Cumbria and Cumberland in the northwest, Welsh *Cymru* (= Wales). The fundamental Welsh adjective *Cymraeg*, 'Welsh, the Welsh language', is in direct descent from the old British adjective *Com-brogicos*. Even the English began to use this label among their various names for the distinct British.

But, despite the Celtic continuity inherent in the whole story of Wales, internal references to groupings smaller than this nationally perceived community, and larger than an individual kindred, are disconcertingly rare and seldom early. So, too, are any incidental allusions to British kingdoms under their actual names. Does this permit the suspicion that the essence of a British state was the dynasty controlling it, and not its territorial extent or label?

As for continuity from Britannia, cities and especially the larger walled former civitas centres might have begun by providing a visible and symbolic focus of power, maintained on supposedly late Roman lines, so long as they were occupied, or occupiable, or could be physically exploited for limited on-site reconstruction. Philip Barker's years of painstaking investigation at Wroxeter (Roman *Viroconium*, the centre of the civitas of the Cornovii) have now revealed the construction well into the 5th century of a large and remarkable timber palace on quasi-Classical lines; presumably this housed a sub-Roman ruler, but we have no idea who he was, or what kingdom was subject to his house. It is also probable that during the same century a similar grandee based himself in part of Roman *Eboracum*, the Brigantian civitas capital at York.

In sources later than Gildas, and markedly so in Wales and southwest England where Roman towns and cities had been least common, rulers tend rather to be associated with periodic re-occupations of the old, pre-Roman, hillforts, or of deserted Roman military bases such as Wroxeter or Gloucester; and this is something on which excavations have been able to throw a little light. There can, however, be some evidence of continuity from Britannia in the matter of names. The early Welsh kingdom of Demetia, or Dyfed – the latter, postally and administratively revived under the British 1974 Local Government Act – more or less corresponds to the Roman civitas of the Demetae in southwest Wales.

How much should be read into the survival of Roman urban place-names (*Londinium*, London, *Corinium*, *Ciren*cester, *Luguvalium*, Car*lisle*) is another matter. The medieval and modern forms have been mediated through Late British and its daughter-languages, or through Old English with appropriate suffixes of the -caster, -chester type taken from Latin *castr-um, -a*; the continuity is not always the same, and not always at once apparent (though 'York' does, tortuously, go back to *Eboracum*). Retention may imply only a public awareness of a town's former existence – not an unbroken occupation. Unfortunately, throughout Celtic Britain, so rich in its several million place-names, the oldest and commonest groups of names are historically far and away the least informative. For example, there are any number of dingles or rural patches or field-sites throughout both Wales and Cornwall, now called (with minor variations) Rhedynog or Redannick. It may feed modern British pride to learn that this form is at least 2,000 years old – it is British *ratinac-o*, 'the place of ferns, or bracken' – but the interest is entirely botanical.

The potency attached to certain British personal names is more useful. When early Welsh kings favoured the name Caratawc – which, as 'Caradog', is still popular in Wales – there must sometimes have been purposeful allusion to Caratacus, the kingly hero who back in the 1st century led a counterattack against the Roman conquest. Betrayed by the pro-Roman queen Cartimandua of the Brigantes, he was paraded in triumph at Rome and, for his impressive bearing and courage, pardoned by the Emperor Claudius. It is scarcely conceivable that so gripping a yarn did not grow into an orally transmitted British epic. Least convincing as any witness of true continuity were the, later, implicit claims by British royal families of a direct descent from their Roman predecessors. By the 8th and 9th centuries, elaborate genealogies purported to trace various native kings from Magnus Maximus, or the great Christian Emperor Constantine I, or Constantine's supposedly British mother Helena. Remoter ancestors were simply given Roman names; much, and often far too much, has been read into their meanings by later historians. It may be misleading for us to read into this, either a conscious nostalgia for a Britain that the Romans had kept free from Saxon invasions, or a latterday need to make a British rule valid through linking it to the last Roman Emperors and usurpers. A great many Britons continued to bear Roman names, including Imperial names, long after 400; and these Britons would be from the families, doubtless hailing from 4th-century senatorial circles in Britannia, which were the progenitors of princes and petty kings. Their emergence was, surely, opportunistic. Power will frequently have grown, as was pointed out earlier, from the possession of large landed estates, the ability to raise an armed following and presumably at some stage the seizure of a suitable, non-urban, stronghold. If – by 600 and later – any such rule was exercised in a framework of Christianity, with kings represented as Christians, and with bishops leading their flocks from royal centres instead of civitas capitals, all this may tell us something about the Church in Celtic Britain; far less about native kingdoms and kingship.

Some kingdom-names have, however, come down to us, along with others, of rarer occurrence, where it is uncertain if they belong to kingdoms of any kind, or just to subsidiary districts and lesser regions. Those in southern Scotland are discussed elsewhere (Chapter 5), but two straddled the present Scotland-England border. A very large state, Rheged, stretched from the southwest Scottish coastal plain (Galloway and Dumfries) across the Lake District (Cumbria) and down into some area of northern Lancashire. Its counterpart region, east of the irregular wide spine of upland Britain, involved southeast Scotland, across the Tweed and certainly Yorkshire. By the 7th century, this contained the two Northumbrian Anglian realms of Bernicia (north) and Deira (south); but, as such, they seem to have been imposed on the extents of corresponding earlier British kingdoms – the northern perhaps called

Bernaccia; the southern, of which York was presumably a major centre, apparently some name close to Deira.

West of Deira, on higher ground and around the modern city of Leeds (itself from an old British district-name, *Loidis*), lay Elmet. Present-day Yorkshire town- and village-names like 'Barwick-in-Elmet' hark back to this. Gildas has a passage in which he addresses five British kings, and he implies that they ruled five mid-6th century kingdoms. Some of these kings, as we shall see, are known independently of Gildas's writing. Among the certain realms are (in Latin) Dumnonia, the southwestern part of Britain, and – as we have seen – Demetia, Dyfed, in southwest Wales, both names being from the titles of former civitates. A third is northwest Wales and Anglesey; its name was Latinized as 'Venedotia', though this is non-Roman and a fresh creation, British *Weneda* – which may have meant something along the lines of 'Desirable Land', as indeed agriculturally this beautiful region still is. Its subsequent Welsh name, revived in 1974 along with Dyfed, is familiar today as Gwynedd.

The fourth kingdom probably lay east of Gwynedd – east of the Welsh river Conwy, in the old district or *cantref* of Rhos, though its original name has not survived. The last, and one of two only with a ruler bearing a Roman instead of British name – Aurelius Caninus – remains geographically most uncertain, though the general area of the Welsh Marches, west Midlands and Severn basin is commonly supposed. Beyond Gildas, other 6th-century kings, not in most cases linked to recognizable kingdoms, figure in early Welsh sources. A similar instance, but this time from the Anglo-Saxon Chronicle, is the record of three kings (Conmail, Condidan and Farinmail) killed when the English took Gloucester, Cirencester and Bath in AD 577.

Where the territorial names are not demonstrably revived from those of former civitates, they appear, like *Weneda*, to be geographical. *Bernaccia* (*Bernicia*) may mean 'Land of the Mountain Passes', apt enough in a region where old roads intersect the hills mainly along valley-sides and valley-floors. *Deira* and *Elmet* have both been proposed as the derivatives of rather earlier forest-names, meaning 'Oak-Forest' and 'Elm-Forest' respectively. We have only the most vague idea as to how the names of internal localities were formed, or continued. Professor Colin Smith makes the interesting point that Bede in 731 cites correctly three Romano-British place-names, all within Elmet, that do not figure in the Classical sources he seems to have known; and which therefore he should have acquired from 'the continuing Latin tradition of the British-speaking Kingdom of Elmet'. By Bede's day this would mean some *written* source, passing from British to Northumbrian Church circles.

The early kings themselves are of interest because they are among the very few named individuals of sub-Roman Celtic Britain. Among Gildas's five, Constantinus and Aurelius Caninus continued the Roman tradition, but the other three are entirely Celtic. They include

20, 21 **Commoners and kings** (*Above*)
Memorial stone of Aliortus, 'a man of Elmet'
(ELMETIACO); 6th century, from Llanaelhaearn,
north Wales. (*Right*) The memorial stone of
King Voteporix of Demetia (Dyfed), mid-6th
century; Ogham inscription around the sides and
top.

Maglocunus of Gwynedd, 'Princely-Hound'; his eastern neighbour
Cuneglasus, 'Tawny-Hound'; and in Demetia, descendant of Irish
chieftains who had come across rather before 400, Voteporix (in British)
or Wotecorix (the corresponding Irish form, in his still-bilingual
kingdom). These are all real men. Maelgwn, to give him his later Welsh
form, figures in various sources. Constantine, if he was also the
Custennin Gorneu ('Constantine-of-Cornwall') in later Welsh, may
indeed be the elderly man whose conversion, or final retreat to some
monastery, is recorded for AD 589. The bilingual tombstone of Voteporix,
whose family chose to describe him by the archaic Roman title of
Protector – by *c*.550 meaningless but no doubt impressive – can still be
seen in a Demetian museum. All these persons are described as
Christians, if in differing degrees backsliders.

Some degree of consciousness of a person's territorial origin, within
Britain, is apparent by the 6th century. Kings and notables, particularly
when possessing a commonly-used name (Constantine is a case in point),
were distinguished in later sources, as they may well have been in
contemporary speech, by epithets of place; military figures and heroes
were often cited as 'of, or from (Somewhere)'. Rather rarely, this occurs
among the several hundred inscribed Christian tombstones dating from
the later 5th century. An important man from Penmachno, in Gwynedd,
has added to his name the words VENEDOTIS CIVE FUIT ('he was a citizen of
Venedotia, *Weneda*'). In the same area, another 6th-century tombstone
describes the dead man as ELMETIACO – the correct Late British adjective,
'an Elmetian'. Here, surely, lies the prototype Yorkshireman in exile;
insisting that, even in death, he be distinguished from feebler folk raised
elsewhere.

Lastly, we can accept that British kingdoms almost certainly did
possess various internal divisions, official or popular; for Wales, they may

have to be postulated as underlying some of those known rather more confidently by the 9th century. In the remote southwest, Cornwall – the final part of the great peninsula, almost cut off by the river Tamar – had a separate Late British name, *Cornouia*, which was Latinized as *Cornubia* and survived as Welsh *Cernyw* and Cornish *Kernow*. Cornwall may have constituted a pagus, a Roman subdivision, within the civitas of the Dumnonii. It reveals further traces of six, putatively very early, internal divisions which (with subsequent further segmentation) had become nine 'hundreds' on the southern English model by Norman times. The Cornish term for any such 'hundred' was *kevran*, originally meaning 'place or district of military assembly'; one of them, Tricurius in a 7th-century Latin source, may be British *Tricorii* ('District of three war-bands'), and another, geographically a quarter of Cornwall west of the cross-peninsular (river Fowey, river Camel) divide, has a name that could come from British *petuaria*, 'a fourth'. We can think here of another early British tribe, the Parisi in east Yorkshire, whose early civitas seems to have been quadripartite, the four parts ranking perhaps as the Roman subdivisions or pagi; one of their settlements, *vicus Petuariensis* (North Ferriby) implies a similar *Petuaria* district-name. The peripheral siting of Cornwall may help to explain any such long survival. Increasingly, too, in southern Scotland and northern England one sees traces of territorial divisions, smaller than a modern administrative county and reflected here and there in occasional place-names, that have to be taken as being non-English; therefore, presumably pre-English, and in some cases reflecting (as in Cornwall) Celtic British arrangements. The impression is that the bare names of the early kingdoms conceal a far more complicated partitioning. It may well be that the only tracts of land at all closely defined, either by measured extent or fixed bounds, *were* these various subdivisions.

Paganism and Christianity

During the 4th century, visitors to the wondrous hot springs and the temple of Sulis Minerva at Aquae Sulis, Bath, wrote (as was customary) various requests to the goddess on small, rolled-up, sheets of lead. Some were thrown into the magical waters. A supplicant named Annianus was particularly vexed, because somebody had pinched six silver coins from his purse. He wanted Sulis to recover his money from this pickpocket, 'whether man or woman, boy or girl, slave or free'; and he added for good measure 'whether pagan or Christian' (*seu gentilis seu cristianus*).

Annianus's tablet reminds us that at this time to be Christian was still only one alternative, and in many people's eyes not necessarily the best. Since 313, Christianity, favoured by the Emperor Constantine the Great and by most of his successors, had been an approved faith. Celtic and Roman Britain had however experienced a long succession of religious choices. The pre-Roman cults had given way to the mixture of Roman and native gods – including non-British native gods who had arrived alongside Germans and other foreigners, serving in the army – and to the specific worship of the deified Emperors. A common dedicatory phrase, too familiar to raise a British eyebrow, was *Numina Augustorum*, 'To the Divine Presences of the Augusti' (the senior Emperors). Britain also became host to various so-called mystery religions which had acquired Roman, or Romanized Greek, followings in Egypt and the Near East: the cults of Isis, of Jupiter Dolichenus, and of Mithras. The contents of some, notably of Mithraism with its male ever-young Divine Hero and its elaborate symbolism and secret liturgies, verged on a real theology. In one light Christianity may be presented as a late Roman Mediterranean mystery religion – similarly rich in detail – that proved to be particularly successful; in the end, almost universally so.

The first Christians in Britannia were individuals during the 2nd and 3rd centuries who had been converted and baptized, as a rule secretly, in some other province – Gaul, or further to the east; despite the Christian revulsion against military service, some may have arrived with the Roman army. Within a population of several millions it would not seem to be possible, archaeologically or historically, to pick them out, and only recently has it become clear how we could begin to do so. The late appearance of exclusively Christian devices and symbols, along with the fact that for some centuries Christians normally met for worship in ordinary domestic buildings, has tended to confine the evidence to the 4th century.

One undoubted stimulus was Christianity's appeal to the population at large. Other religions might be exclusive in the extreme; Mithraism, with its male secrecy and financial commitments, seems to have been the preserve of government, mercantile and military circles. The Christian faith by its nature, linked as it was to the central Gospel message, reached out to rich and poor, men and women, free and unfree alike. Salvation without any price-tag was assured to all those admitted through baptism and confirmation. Before Galerian's Edict of 311, and the Edict of Milan in 313, affirming Imperial sponsorship, there had been many phases of persecution. The main charge against Christians lay not in their religion itself, which from 260 had been *religio licita* – a 'permitted religion' – but in their strict devotion to One God; and thus their unwillingness, in contrast to the followers of most other faiths, to acknowledge either the Gods of Rome or the deified Emperors. This, in Roman thought, did not just point to subversion; it endangered the balance between the Gods and men, and therefore Rome's very stability.

The extent of Christianity in 4th-century Britannia can be shown with a distribution map, provided we realize that not all the pieces of evidence have equal weight, and that this should be indicated. A church, or cemetery, offers far stronger witness for the practice of Christianity at a given locality than would the mere finding of one or two unquestionably

Christian trinkets that a traveller may have chanced to drop. The map shows a general spread throughout England and Wales, but it also hints that both town and countryside were involved. The organization of Christianity followed that of civil government; Christian communities were, expectedly, thickest in towns, where any such community (*ecclesia*) was headed by its bishop. The metropolitans – whom we would now call archbishops – ruled the Church from the centres of prefectures. Some of the Christian vocabulary originated in the Greek-speaking provinces of the east, Greek words being taken into Latin; *angelus* (angel), *diaconus* (deacon), *ecclesia* (Christian flock; later, a church) and *episcopus* (bishop) began as Greek words for 'messenger', 'servant', 'assembly' and 'overseer'. Other terms, still in use – like 'diocese', and 'vicar' – derive immediately from the vocabulary of Roman civil administration.

British bishops are first recorded in the attendance-list of a Council held at Arles in 314; the names of their seats probably represent, in Britannia, the cities of York, London, Lincoln and – it is assumed – Cirencester. If so, these were the centres of the four provinces into which Britannia Superior and Inferior were split in the 4th century. Taking the better-documented progressions in other parts of the Roman empire as a guide, we can argue that after 314, step by step, each British civitas (some twenty or more) had its own bishop. Within most if not all civitas capitals there would have been at least one church – either the bishop's congregational church inside the city walls, and/or others, beginning as funerary chapels, sited in the Christian portions of the cemeteries which by Roman law had to exist outside the city limits.

It would be completely erroneous to think that, if Roman Britain was mainly pagan up to 400, the Britain of sub-Roman times rapidly adopted Christianity. When the conversion of the English kingdoms began early in the 7th century, it is likely that a substantial percentage of the British race was by then Christian; it is doubtful whether it was universally so. The higher flights of Christian thought and argument lacked the direct appeal of simple faith, and in any case the supporting literature and commentaries were accessible only to those educated in spoken and written Latin (and, sometimes, Greek). Fourth-century Christianity in Roman Britain is full of interest because, in a strange way, many of its manifestations seem to bear a distinctively British imprint. To some extent this can be said (Chapter 7) of Christianity in later Celtic Britain and Ireland – where, by the way, those popular phrases 'the Celtic Church' and 'Celtic Christianity' must, in view of the universality of Christianity, be deplored as being both misleading and inaccurate. Annianus's lead *defixio* at Bath, with his appeal to the potent goddess Sulis Minerva, should remind us that in the last century of Roman Britannia the Christian faith co-existed with vigorous paganism.

This can be well shown from the most striking of archaeological finds – some of the splendid hoards, all fairly recently recovered. *Durobrivae*

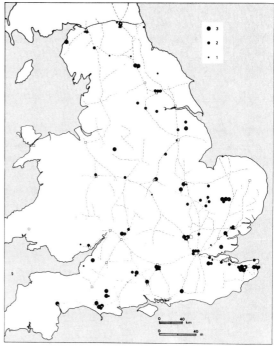

22–24 The spread of Christianity
(*Right*) Distribution of evidence for
Christianity in late Roman Britain; of
the symbols, 3 indicates virtually
certain evidence, 2 reasonably
probable, and 1 no more than possible.
(*Below left*) Part of the Water Newton
hoard, early 4th century: gold votive
plaques, in a pagan tradition, bearing
the Christian chi–rho monogram.
(*Below right*) A purely pagan silver
votive plaque, inscribed to Mars, from
Barkway, Hertfordshire.

55

('the fort-of-bridges') began as an early Roman fort on the river Nene, at Water Newton west of Peterborough. The name was then transferred to a larger walled town in the middle of a rich farming district, a town that could briefly have served as a civitas centre. In 1975, a spectacular group of gold and silver objects was unearthed; it has since been acquired by the British Museum, cleaned, restored, published and put on display.

This hoard, among the most important Late Roman Christian assemblages anywhere, has a range of silver vessels; some are inscribed in Latin, and some show a characteristic Christian device called the *chi-rho*. It is a monogram of the Greek capital letters *chi* (a sound like our 'K') and *rho* ('R'), the first two letters of *Christos* – 'the Anointed One: Christ', and was traditionally promoted by Constantine I after 313. The chi-rho is often flanked by the first and last Greek letters – *alpha* ('A') and *omega* (the long 'O' sound, which is written something like 'W'): they refer to a passage in Revelations, i.8, or xxi.6, 'I am Alpha and Omega, saith the Lord God . . . I am . . . the beginning and the end.'

Among the vessels are two jugs and a wine-strainer (Roman wines contained coarse sediments), a large dish with prominent chi-rho, a hanging-lamp bowl, and four small cups or bowls, one with two handles like a later chalice. They represent a service of plate for the Christian Communion. Not all the objects need be of similar date; several had been mended, or were worn. Most of them should however belong between AD 300 and 325. Circumstances suggest they were bundled up and buried in a town garden or back plot within Durobrivae around 350.

But if this was the church plate of the local ecclesia, hidden at a moment of dire emergency, it was accompanied by a series of small, ribbed sheet-silver, triangular plaques; several are gilded and some have sheet-gold appliqué discs. Most bear chi-rhos with or without A and W, and most have small holes indicating that they were strung from or pinned to a backdrop – from which they must have been torn, hastily, to be concealed with the vessels. Votive plaques (as these are called) resembling stylized feathers and fronds, in silver or bronze, were typically non-Christian; rich devotees might buy them at shrines and temples, where plaques would display names, attributes and crude pictures of the deities involved, and arrange for them to be displayed in connection with a request or vow. One of the Durobrivae plaques reads (above a chi-rho disc) 'Iamcilla has fulfilled the vow which she promised'; and the Latin phrase (*votum quod promisit*) is also found in pagan transactions. In this Romano-British town – and what sort of earlier building may have become a Christian temple? – the Faith had not entirely freed itself from older habits.

Nor, nearer 400, were those older ways entirely in decline. The more recent (1979) treasure from Thetford, Norfolk, also to be seen in the British Museum, is just as spectacular. It is best explained as the stock of a merchant or jeweller, concealed or stolen for hiding about 380–90. The

81 objects of gold, silver, and precious stones include 33 silver spoons, all save two inscribed with personal names like Auspicius and Silviola, or with dedications to a pagan deity. He is *Faunus* – the old Roman god of the agricultural landscape and woodlands, equated with the Greeks' Pan. The Thetford inscriptions follow his name with subsidiary Celtic (Latinized British) titles: in Professor Kenneth Jackson's readings, *Medugenos*, 'Mead-begotten'; *Blatucus*, 'Bringer of flowers (or corn)'; and *Ausicus*, 'Long-ear, Prick-ear' (remember Pan's hooves and little horns). What this means – the commissioning of such inscribed spoons, the religious habits of those who wanted them – is open to discussion; but here, a well-supported cult of Faunus flourished at the very end of Roman Britain, and perhaps in East Anglia, a region where urban and rural Christianity was well represented. Very similar conclusions must accompany the evidence (mostly from dated coin hoards) that locally active pagan temples were to be found in many parts of 4th-century Britannia. There are, of course, those who claim that the 'Old Faith' comprising these native and Roman cults never wholly vanished, but grumbled away stubbornly in the background of post-Roman and medieval Christianity. Various horned gods of the hunt, of stock-raising and aggressive fertility, like *Coccidius* and *Belatucadros* (equated with the Romans' Mars and Silvanus), united in the demon-figure of witchcraft through the Middle Ages. Chapter 7 will however explore the progress of Christianity.

Merchants from afar

Finally, we may glance at a less familiar aspect of sub-Roman Britain which, in a mainly historical approach, rests decidedly on archaeology. Steady research among the (literally) tons of pottery found in Romano-British excavations has shown that, besides the familiar Gaulish samian ware and the endless variations of coarse wares made in Britannia, there are late Roman imports of exotic character. There are distinctive pots from the Rhineland, northern Gaul, Italy and North Africa. Most of these were imported cross-Channel, previous handling being overland to the European Channel harbours; and some are a little after 400. Correspondingly, Britannia's 4th-century bronze coinage came largely from Continental mints, at first Trier, later Arles and Lyon. The trade nexus involving France, Germany and England was not properly resumed (but then in a very similar form) until the 13th and 14th centuries.

Excavated sites in western Britain and Ireland proper to the 5th to 8th centuries AD, unlike their earlier Romano-British counterparts, lack permanent masonry structures or much pottery, and frequently possess destructively acid soils that can dissolve metalwork and bones. None the less, since the 1930s, the occurrence on such sites of several varieties of wheel-made pottery, vaguely 'Roman' in style but attributable neither to

Roman Britain nor to any local manufactories, has led to the belief that these were long-distance imports by sea. Two such classes (those known as D and E) are referred, without specific detail, to post-Roman western France, and are discussed elsewhere (Chapter 5). The remainder is dominated by the largest group, class B, all wheel-made containers for liquids (or occasionally, perhaps, olives). There is an associated class A – the red-slipped or colour-coated dishes and bowls of continuing Roman and Hellenistic character.

It has transpired that these kinds of pottery – whose importance on British and Irish sites resides in the fact that, often, they may be the *only* finds capable of being approximately dated – are the same as others known elsewhere by such titles as North African (or Phocaean) Red Slip ware, Ballana Type 6, Sardis jars, and so on. Discoveries in Britain involve, more often than not, a mere handful of stray sherds, unlike the hundredweights – complete vessels among them – at such places as Carthage or Caesarea.

The demonstration of this transfer of material, ranging from the Isles of Scilly to Scotland's Western Isles, from Cork and Kerry up to Antrim and Down, has been a minor triumph for British and Irish students. Not all the North African or Mediterranean sources have yet been identified, but it is clear that class B refers to large-scale commercial production. In the case of class A, fairly rapid changes in shape and ornament has meant that the home-based time span of many given dish and bowl types can be tied down to a half-century or rather less. Such close dating, allowing a short lag in time, could theoretically be transferred to British and Irish findspots.

The inferences to be won from all this are another matter. Obviously, these pots came in ships. But in how many, and from where? Why did they sail so far? Was there any reciprocal trade, and if so, in what commodities? Were the pots and their much more important and desirable contents the primary cargo, or were they space-fillers in ships plying for quite different ends?

Only outline answers can be provided. No classes A and B imports ought to have arrived before about 450 and many are consistent with shipments a little later, up to about 530. The agencies may have been trading craft owned by institutions or by their captains, plying in summer out of the great ports of Classical antiquity – Carthage, Alexandria and Tarsus. All class B containers are amphoras, handled jars large and small, mostly suitable for wine, though some very large (Bv) cylindrical vessels from what is now Tunisia are otherwise associated with olive oil in bulk. The class A fine wares are, by comparison, secondary items – afterthoughts and space-fillers.

The motives behind the few voyages necessarily represented are related to trade, mainly because trading ships are the most likely to have been involved. Britannia had a reputation as the source of certain

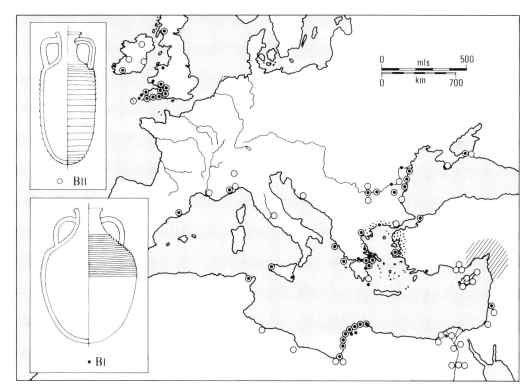

25 The approximate distribution of class Bi and Bii amphoras. Stippling (around the Aegean) shows the area of likely origin of Bi; cross-hatching (Antioch and hinterland?) of Bii.

products, some of them slightly rarified: high-quality woollen garments, and prized hunting-dogs. More practically, it had been an Imperially-controlled source of tin and lead, and there had been British pewter-ware manufactories. Though references to any kind of marine contact are rare in early British and Irish sources (and tend in general to point towards Gaul) there is one odd tale in the early 7th-century life of an Egyptian bishop and saint, where a captain from Alexandria, his craft laden with corn, is carried away by storms as far as Britain and is able to barter his cargo upon landfall, half for coinage and half for tin. In Cornwall the production of small tin ingots smelted from alluvially-won cassiterite – what is called 'tin-streaming' – was a cottage industry that almost certainly went on long after the 4th century. In the Mendip Hills of Somerset, lead ores were easily won; pewter-making (pewter is an alloy of lead and tin) may have occurred after 400 in Dumnonia. Finds of the Mediterranean classes A and B pottery are concentrated in the southwest, and along the Bristol Channel coasts.

Wine was a conspicuous luxury, proper to sub-Roman rulers and war-leaders (there are sherds of class B at South Cadbury Castle). It was closer to being a liturgical necessity in the Christian celebration of the

Mass. The attractive little block-stamped motifs on some class A dishes come from the repertory of late-Classical and symbolic Christian art, with peacocks, doves, dolphins, lambs, palm-fronds and small outline Christian crosses. Few clear instances are recorded, but we may imagine that Britons were among the many hardy pilgrims to the Holy Places, the Egyptian deserts and the great New Testament localities of the Levant. From the 4th century, these pilgrims travelled by paying their way, bedroll under one arm and a satchel of provisions under the other, on whatever commercial shipping would take human deck-cargo at its own risk. If a sea trip could be horrendous, at least it was free from the bandits, battles and plagues associated with overland travel.

Where men and women can fare as pilgrims for Christ or as individual adventurers, other things can fare along with them – small objects of art and virtu as souvenirs, books and writings, and above all new *ideas*. The presence of these Mediterranean luxuries in sub-Roman Britain, as in Ireland, suggests that certain fresh notions in religion and art, themselves unlikely to be legacies from Roman Britannia, may have been introduced in this way. Their importance can be over-emphasized, but the transmarine contact seems genuine enough. It is a useful reminder that, isolated from Rome in the turmoils of the 5th century, Celtic Britain was still accessible by sea and that fresh links, not always immediately to and from Gaul, could slowly come into being.

26, 27 **The Mediterranean connection** (*Top*) Basal stamps on fragments of Phocean (Asia Minor) Red Slip ware dishes found at Tintagel, Cornwall, late 5th to mid-6th century. (*Centre*) Stamps on the same ware found in the Mediterranean. (*Below*) North African (Carthage area) Red Slip ware dish found at Tintagel, 6th century. Diameter 27 cm.

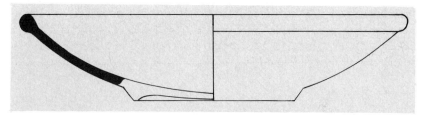

4·Early Cornwall

THE SOUTHWESTERN British kingdom or principality that emerged from the end of Roman Britain and is now the administrative county of Cornwall owes most of its history to its geographical position. A long sea-girt peninsula with a central spine of granite uplands, it has a single land frontier with the rest of Britain, the southern third of which consists of the broad reaches and estuary of the river Tamar. Though there is evidence for a period of Roman military occupation in the later 1st century, this was not apparently followed by any effective civil presence. Within the canton of Dumnonia, stretching from the Somerset Levels all the way to Land's End, the territory beyond Isca Dumnoniorum (Exeter) was left to its native ways. The principal, perhaps the only, Roman interest lay in the peninsula's mineral resources. Tin, an essential component of the alloys pewter and bronze, has been sought by deep shaft-mining since Tudor times; but during prehistory, when the technologies required to dig and tunnel through granite and hard-rock country were unavailable, stream-tin (nodules of cassiterite) could only be won by clearing, shovelling and washing the alluvial gravels. These lay in the bottoms of many wooded valleys, the courses of streams draining laterally from high moors inland where tin-bearing lodes or ore-bodies intersected the surface.

This tin industry, involving traditional knowledge and about the same degree of rough carpentry skills as that associated with the 19th-century gold rushes in North America, went back to the Bronze Age. By pre-Roman times it must have reached an adequate if static level, and we can imagine small family concerns, working their valley pitches. Little irregular pits in the wet gravels may have been planked or shored, separation would have been by water-washing and manual sorting, and the tin grains, smelted with charcoal, ended as surprisingly pure ingots, cast in open stone moulds.

Rome was particularly concerned with the smelting of lead, which was the source for most water-pipes (and, in later centuries, coffins and large caskets), and the main component in pewter; lead ores could also yield limited quantities of silver. In the 3rd and 4th centuries, a period when Spanish tin-production was threatened by civil unrest and other difficulties and when demands for household pewter-ware had greatly increased, Cornish tin production was probably encouraged to expand; it may have been subject to taxes and to some degree of Imperial control (for example, pre-emption of much of the output). Southwest Britain in

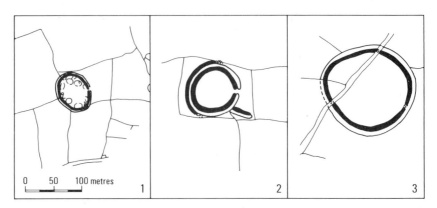

0   50   100 metres

1   2   3

28–30 **The Cornish Iron Age tradition** (*Above*) Outline plans of 'rounds' or
univallate defended farmsteads, Late Iron Age and Roman Cornwall. 1 Trethurgy
near St Austell, 2 Lower Helland near Bodmin, 3 Little Delinuth near Camelford.
(*Below*) Stone-walled oval huts in the small village of Chysauster, occupied from
about 100 BC to AD 400. (*Opposite*) The Rumps, a north-Cornish promontory fort
with three ramparts guarding the neck.

general shared in this new importance. The Mendip lead mines, surface pits in the easily worked limestone, adjoined mining villages like Charterhouse-on-Mendip, and at nearby Camerton there was a whole settlement of pewterers. These circumstances go far to explain why – despite the absence of any general Romanization – Roman pottery and small objects and, above all, coins are relatively common from the Tamar westward to Scilly. Coin hoards, particularly of the late 3rd and 4th centuries, have been found in circumstances that suggest not so much circulation in a region with a markedly non-monetary economy, but official payments for tin. Coins were then simply hidden as potential wealth. Silver was, after all, silver in any shape; and bronze coinage might even be recycled, as with a clumsy disc-brooch from the Isles of Scilly that some enthusiast tried to make out of a 2nd-century sestertius.

Tinning apart, the picture of Roman-period Cornwall (and at least part of Devon) is one of a continuing native Iron Age region involved in agriculture and stock-raising. The commonest settlement-site is the 'round', or small embanked enclosure – a straightforward farm, with houses or huts standing within an immediate yard, encircled by small and prehistoric-looking fields. Similar but unenclosed settlements – single homes and hamlets, the 'open' sites – are also known, often on sandy coasts. The farm enclosures, 600 or 700 of them in Cornwall alone, arose by the 2nd century BC from earlier (even from Bronze Age) prototypes, and were demonstrably in use until at least AD 500, well into Celtic British times. If roads or customary routes existed, they would have followed the lines of prehistoric trackways-of-convenience, and are now beneath modern roads and country lanes. A scatter of rough, if genuine, late Roman milestones west of Exeter tells us only of slight administrative interest in major routes leading to natural harbours; there is no trace of any extension of the full Roman road system. Lastly, the intensive fieldwork of recent decades shows us that here, as elsewhere, population densities have been much underestimated. It can be no more than an informed guess, but the population of 4th-century Cornwall could have been around 40,000 (it is now ten times that figure).

The origins of Cornwall

Southwest Britain constituted the territory of the Dumnonii, but implicit in later Roman geography is the presence of an internal sub-grouping, the Cornovii. Tribes of the same name are known from the Shropshire-Cheshire area, and also from Caithness in northeast Scotland. There is no reason to connect these two northerly groups ethnically with each other, or either with the presumed Cornovii of *Durocornovium* ('fort of the Cornovii'), an as yet unlocated site somewhere west of the river Tamar. The British word *corn-* ('horn') may refer here to followers of the cult of some pagan horned god, or to a geographical feature. In Cornwall, these were conceivably the spectacular coastal 'horns' or fortified promontories, the cliff-castles favoured as defensive settlements during Iron Age and Roman times. It can be argued, as we noted in Chapter 3, that what is now Cornwall could have been distinguished in Romanized British as *Cornouia*, land of the Cornovii; in the later and purely Latin guise, *Cornubia*, this emerges as Cornwall's name through 8th-century writings. The still later 'Cornwall' contains the root-word as its first syllable; the second part is the generic Anglo-Saxon word for the British, *Walas* or *wealas* (as in Wales, Welsh), and 'Cornwall' is thus a compressed hybrid term signifying 'the land of the Britons of *Corn[-ouia, -ubia]*'.

As a distinctive part of Celtic Britain, the former *civitas Dumnoniorum* possesses an extremely ill-documented history in post-Roman times. It was an area of British speakers. The evolution of a regional dialect (Late

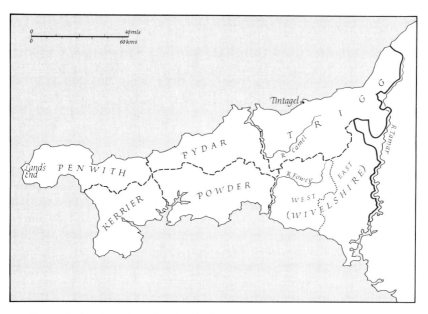

31 Cornwall, the six ancient 'hundreds' with their modern names. In southeast Cornwall, opposite Plymouth, the original Cornish name of the Anglo-Saxons' 'two-fold-shire', now East and West (Wivelshire), has been lost.

Southwestern British) into its successive stages of Primitive, Old and Middle Cornish, and the retention of this non-English vernacular in its west Cornish fastnesses almost until Victorian times, went a long way to characterize – in English eyes – the separateness of a poor and marginal region. Full incorporation of Cornwall within modern England was in some ways a post-medieval process. It was hastened by the rise of Cornish copper and tin mining in the 17th and 18th centuries, a rise associated with an early, important, and localized industrial revolution and with a band of native inventors and scientists (Davy, Trevithick, Gilbert, etc.). It was consolidated only when the 19th-century railway system, conceived firstly in terms of an industrial service, reached Penzance and laid the foundations of the Cornish tourist boom. Yet it may well be another century before most native Cornish cease to think, subconsciously and automatically, in terms of 'Cornwall' and 'England', an Us-and-Them syndrome sharpened by distance from central government and, recently, by post-war revivals of a Cornish national-consciousness movement.

Kings of Dumnonia
Looking back, even for most general guidance, at the early histories of Scotland and Wales, we are led to think of a model of post-Roman Dumnonia involving the rise of a native kingdom and – in view of the extended nature of the region – subsidiary fiefdoms within it. The relevant historical sources are few, have survived in late (i.e., medieval)

65

sources and come to us mostly via Wales. If there was any one major centre of early literacy in Dumnonia, we remain ignorant of its nature, location and products. However, there *are* clear indications of a Dumnonian king-list, surviving through tradition and by Welsh interests. It names a succession, doubtless incomplete, of rulers from the late 5th (or early 6th) century to about the 9th and not a few of the persons named are independently attested at the correct periods. Medieval Welsh genealogies necessarily present king-lists as family trees, but there is no reason to suppose that the Dumnonian list does not contain its share of genuine father-to-son, or uncle-to-nephew, sequences.

There are two important points here. First, there is a special southwest dimension, because this period spanned the great migrations to Armorica (Brittany). Accepting Professor Jackson's linguistic conclusions, it was a broadly based, all-Dumnonian draught, with emigrants anywhere from Dorset to Land's End, as the initial phase, and in a second wave the exodus may have been mainly from Cornwall. It is unlikely, but it is not inconceivable, that Dumnonian rulers regarded themselves (and were regarded) from time to time as exercising kingship on both sides of the English Channel; so that we have the problem of similar or identical names in both British and Breton sources. Secondly, the compression of post-Roman Dumnonia – militarily and politically by the advance of the English and their later kingdom of Wessex, in terms of language and native culture by the spread of the English speech – occurred at an uncertain rate in one direction: westwards. Dumnonian territory shrank eventually to the land west of the Tamar (Cornwall), and if there were any claimants to native kingship as late as the 9th century, their realm would have been even smaller: at most, the four western 'hundreds', or Cornwall west of the river Fowey–river Camel line. Because of this long politico-geographical fluidity, it is hard to detect any Dumnonian capital, or any fixed, continuously maintained royal centre. Rather as among the component kingdoms of early Scotland, the picture is one of a series of seats or citadels occupied only for limited periods. The old Roman civitas centre, Exeter, at the intersection of a main route westwards and the first upstream narrowings of the river Exe, was abandoned during the 5th century. Its revived and limited (religious) re-occupation two centuries later was an Anglo-Saxon event.

Any attempt to pin down Dumnonian kings to known localities must be based upon archaeological, epigraphic and inferential clues; the written sources give little aid. Fifth-century figures can be (as elsewhere) semi-legendary; like Cynan (or Conan) Meriadoc, a leader in the migrations to Brittany – or, from one of the genealogies, his father Eudaf Hen ('Old Eudaf'), who typifies the usual claim of ultimate descent from a Last-Days-of-Roman-Britain grandee. In another pedigree, 'Eudaf' is also father of the Romano-British princess Helen, the entirely legendary mother of the Emperor Constantine the Great.

However, there is no objection to a later sequence, from Tudwal (three generations from Conan) to Geraint. Cynfawr son of Tudwal, or *Cunomorus* ('Hound-of-the-Sea'), is either a British king ruling in Armorica mentioned in early 6th-century Continental sources, or the *Cunomorus* named on the Castle Dore inscribed stone (see below) from 6th-century Cornwall; or, improbably, both. His son Custennin, whose name in Latin would have been *Constantin(us)*, can be equated with the ruler of Dumnonia addressed in Gildas's 6th-century writings. Constantine is a not uncommon personal name in Celtic Britain and one Welsh source calls him Custennyn *Gorneu* (where *Corneu* is a specialized epithet, meaning 'of-Cornwall').

Constantine's son is named as Erbin, and Erbin's as Geraint or Gereint. Given the time-scale, he may be the *Gereint rac deheu* ('Gereint for the South') in the list of British heroes assembled against the Northumbrian Angles around 600, included in the *Gododdin* poem. This particular personal name seems to have had some inherent heroic quality. Celtic in origin, in its Romanized form of Gerontius it was borne by the British general, *magister militum*, who during 409 rebelled with his forces in Spain against the usurping Emperor Constantine III, and – finally stolen by the English! – it occurs as that of the central figure in Cardinal Newman's poem and Elgar's oratorio, *The Dream of Gerontius*. There are traces of a heroic saga (partly in verse) about a Geraint who fell in battle against the English at *Llongborth*, perhaps Langport in Somerset. It is however likely that he was a second Gereint, not the son of Erbin, but a later king against whom, as the Anglo-Saxon Chronicle recorded, Ine king of Wessex fought in 710. Five years earlier, as 'Geruntius, king of Domnonia', he had been the recipient of a long letter from Aldhelm, the West Saxon abbot of Malmesbury and first bishop of Sherborne.

Subsequent kings, known only by name, float in time, space and ancestry. For example, we could guess that the *Dumnarth rex Cerniu* whose drowning is recorded for the year 875 in the *Annales Cambriae* is also the 'Doniert' who, as an inscription on a 9th-century east-Cornwall cross-shaft tells us, ordered it to be carved and set up for the sake of his soul. Even later is a carved stone cross of about AD 1000 from Penzance in the very west of Cornwall, one inscribed panel of which has been read as *regis + ricati crux* – 'The cross of King Ricatus'. Unless Ricatus was a latter-day megalomaniac, his realm can hardly have amounted to anything more than a Land's End barony.

Such are the bare historical or externally documented bones, the skeletal evidence that there *was* a Celtic British kingdom of Dumnonia, physically diminished ever-westwards into *Cernyw*, as the Welsh called distant Cornwall. However, three other lines of evidence are known and must be considered. One, distinctly enigmatic, takes us back to the matter of Cornwall's internal divisions (Chapter 3). The significance of their place-names was mentioned in another context. The origin of the Saxon

32, 33 **Chieftains in post-Roman Dumnonia** (*Left*) The 6th-century *Men Scryfys* ('written stone') in the Land's End peninsula – it commemorates RIALOBRANUS, whose name begins with *ri(g)alo-*, 'royal, kingly'. (*Right*) The Doniert Stone, near Liskeard, may have been set up by 'Dumnarth rex Cerneu id est Cornubiae', a late 9th-century king named in an early Welsh source.

English 'hundred' has given rise to much discussion, but it is generally supposed that, as a land-division, a hundred was an area capable of supporting enough families to provide when necessary one hundred fighting-men. The Welsh equivalent, the *cantref*, is obviously the same thing, because this word is a compound of *cant*, 'hundred', and *tref*, 'farmstead, agricultural tenement'. The Cornish word for the Cornish hundred is *kevran*, cognate with Welsh *cyfranc* ('meeting, armed encounter') and Breton *coufranc* ('muster, dispute'); and the sense of *kevran* could thus be '(area for) an armed muster; an obligatory recruiting-district'. One of the original hundred-names, that of the once-tripartite Trigg, was the same as that of the Gaulish tribe of the *Tricorii*. In other words, it implied a district proper to a threefold armed levy, or to the mustering of three war-bands.

Are these survivals from pre-Roman Dumnonia, or do they indicate immediately post-Roman arrangements? Were such muster-calls last invoked against the Roman army in the AD 60s, or were they maintained in the background until Gildas's civil wars of the 5th century, and the English victories in the lower Severn area in the late 6th? It seems most improbable that, even in the less-Romanized half of the *civitas Dumnoniorum*, Rome would have encouraged the perpetuation of a district-based, armed levy, system.

The legendary past

Our next point takes us into a discussion, not of the historical Dumnonian kings mentioned already, but of a parallel world that we glimpse in legend and literature instead of in chronicles and pedigrees. These two worlds will of course have touched at many places, as when the real King Geraint, alive in 705 and killed in 710 (or thereabouts), became the subject of a lost Celtic saga fragmentarily preserved in the much later *Black Book of Carmarthen*; was named in a Welsh triad as one of the Three Seafarers of the Island of Britain; and was thought suitable to partner the fair Enid in the medieval Welsh romance, *Gereint vab Erbin*.

Here, as Oliver Padel's researches are making clear, there must have been a substantial corpus of purely Dumnonian legend – much of it concerned with kings and princes and heroines and castles – that persisted strongly into Norman times, and must have been transmitted orally in Old and Middle Cornish. Presumably, in common with the rest of Celtic Britain, there were 'Arthur' stories, resting on a general belief in a 5th-century war-leader (*not* a territorial king) who had opposed the coming of the Saxons. The countless Arthurian localities in southwest Britain, natural features or prehistoric monuments, go back to this strain. Distinct from this, and confined to Dumnonia, we can begin to glimpse native rulers who figure in Lives of Saints rather than pedigrees, like the

7th-century Cado and the still later Teudar. In particular there was a tale of epic, almost Greek-tragedy, proportions, subsequently taken up by Norman and other poets and handed over to European literature – the drama of the Tragic Lovers, with King Mark, the young Tristan and the beautiful Iseult, a tale which, there are very strong reasons for thinking, is wholly Cornish in origin.

It is today immaterial to enquire whether these were real people of early British history. The point is that Dumnonians believed they had been, and in this particular belief there was a legible inscribed stone standing near Fowey for all to read, saying DRUSTANUS HIC IACIT CUNOMORI FILIUS – 'Drustanus lies here, the son of Cunomorus'. *Drustan* is the familiar Tristan. The historical king Cunomorus was, according to the Breton 10th-century Life of St Pol (de Leon, the west Cornish bishop Paul), also called Mark or Marcus, *quem alio nomine Quonomorium vocant*, 'whom men call by another name, Quonomorius', and who was known as a powerful monarch of Dumnonia. Here, then, stood public authentication – names of the king who sought a young bride, and the son (later deflected to the less embarrassing relationship of nephew) who, sent to escort Iseult back to Cornwall, so unhappily fell in love with her. Iseult (*Esselt*) is itself a Cornish name originating, Kenneth Jackson suggests, in a British *Adsiltia*, 'She-who-must-be-gazed-upon', an exact match to the Latin 'Miranda'.

34, 35 Castle Dore, traditional seat of King Mark (*Top*) Inscribed 6th-century granite pillar from the site. It reads (with some reversed and ligatured letters) DRUSTANUS HIC IACIT CUNOMORI FILIUS. Early medieval Cornish may have interpreted this as pointing to the grave of Tristan, son of King Mark (Marcus Cunomorus). (*Above*) The Early Iron Age fort, which has traces of apparent post-Roman occupation.

Tintagel

When that ingenious Welshman, Geoffrey of Monmouth, drew together countless strands of British history (real or supposed) for his 12th-century *History of the Kings of Britain*, his debt to the Cornish remnants of Dumnonian legend was considerable. Geoffrey's own eternal-triangle romance, featuring King Uther Pendragon, Gorlois duke of Cornwall, and Igerna his wife whose beauty so unfortunately caught the eye of Uther, was set in the most romantic of all Dumnonian citadels – the sea-girt crag of Tintagel. It was here that the king, magically transformed by Merlin into the likeness of the absent and soon-to-be-slain Gorlois, was able to have his way with Igerna; thus becoming the father of King Arthur, and by so doing enriching not only subsequent English literature but every shopkeeper in the modern Tintagel area.

And here, peering through the pre-Raphaelite mists, the mighty strains of Wagnerian opera, Tennyson's *Idylls* and the literary accretions of centuries, we encounter solid ground. There *were* Dumnonian royal seats, archaeologically as real as the citadels of early Scotland. If Marcus Cunomorus lived anywhere in the neighbourhood of his son's tombstone (and grave), then the re-occupied Iron Age hillslope fort of Castle Dore is the obvious candidate. Dr Ralegh Radford's pre-war excavations of the interior, deeply disturbed by centuries of ploughing, revealed the last traces of a rectangular timber hall with ancillary structures – if not firmly dated, then certainly not inconsistent with a 5th–6th century use. Throughout Dumnonia such re-used hillforts, as Dr Ian Burrow and Professor Philip Rahtz have demonstrated, constitute the major group of sites attributable to post-Roman occupation (this is inferred from finds, evidence of re-fortification and direct historical involvements). Among the total should lie other Castle Dores, awaiting discovery.

Tintagel (the name is pronounced Tin-*taj*-ell) is still the most spectacular, if also now the most problematic. Standing on a once-remote stretch of the north Cornish coast, it is a high protruding headland whose slate neck – fallen away to a narrow saddle with a modern concrete bridge – just prevents it from becoming a true offshore island. On the east side there is a landing-beach, lashed with breakers during stormy high water, but in calm conditions a sheltered haven and one in use until recently for the loading of quarried slates into small coastal vessels. The place-name is Cornish: *dyn*, a fortress, and *tagell*, a neck or constriction.

On the landward side, towering over this neck, stand the castellated remains of a double-ward medieval castle, and there is a smaller corresponding ward on the so-called Island. Though often said to be the work of Reginald, earl of Cornwall, in the 12th century, most of what is now visible is perhaps more safely attributed to Earl Richard in the 13th. Over most of the island, after one passes through the small inner ward, are to be seen clusters of small rectangular slate-walled rooms or huts, described as the component buildings of a Celtic monastery. These were excavated (and their walls reconstructed) in the 1930s. Turn-of-the-century photographs suggest that the little buildings, if low and ruinous, were then just visible in the short turf. One cluster (site A) contains a narrow 12th- and 13th-century chapel; a curious position, since the chapels of medieval castles are normally inside the walls.

The reasons for interpreting all these non-Castle structures as the components of a monastery include the general remoteness of Tintagel, and the discovery in and around most of the walls of a very large quantity (thousands of individual sherds) of the Mediterranean imported wine-jars, dishes and oil-containers described in Chapter 3, datable to the 5th,

36, 37 **Tintagel, as photographed in about 1900** (*Left*) The east interior of the medieval chapel on the Island, showing plain granite altar-top. (*Above*) A view showing the general cragginess and isolation.

6th and early 7th centuries. The arguments now raised *against* this explanation are numerous. Unlike the dozen or so known pre-Norman monasteries in Cornwall, Tintagel possesses no documentation in this role, figures in no saint's life and has no continuous Christian tradition. As for the field archaeology, there is no monastic cemetery (the few graves found by the chapel could be medieval or later), no trace of a church older than the 12th-century remains, and few if any of the usual ancillary structures. The total of identified 'monastic cells', single, in clusters or in alignments, has now risen through 1976–81 fieldwork and the exposures caused by a 1983 surface fire from around thirty to over a hundred. Many of them closely recall in plan, size and details the one-roomed homes of Cornwall and Devon between the 12th and 14th centuries; and since post-Roman monastic cells elsewhere are generally much smaller and of circular plan, the answer seems to be that the Tintagel 'cells' *are* mostly medieval and go with Earl Richard's castle (as barracks, or a subordinate defended village, or lodgings for a retinue).

73

38 The Romantic view of Tintagel in a 19th-century engraving.

Assuming that the finds – mostly imported pottery – proper to the 5th–7th-centuries AD use of Tintagel really belong to less substantial but as yet unrecognized buildings below the stone-walled clusters, how do we interpret this remarkable place?

Without further excavation certainty is impossible; but it can be suggested that what we have here is a major Dumnonian royal seat –

possibly the chief among such places, until the 7th century – and that its selection for this purpose in the early or mid-5th century had something to do with its status in the Roman period. For this must surely be the Romano-British *Durocornovium*. The name is contained (in a 7th-century compilation, the Ravenna Cosmography) within a route-sequence going west from Exeter. As Professors Leo Rivet and Colin Smith point out, with the exception of Exeter all the places named in it must have been minor, in Roman terms. It is possible that they were derived from some earlier list kept for administrative purposes, not from any straight succession along a road system; and two of them (with the suffix -*statio*) are probably tax-gathering offices. Going west, *Durocornovium* comes just after *Tamara*, which must be a Roman post on the river Tamar; Tintagel lies less than 20 miles west of the Tamar crossing at Launceston. Nor are actual Roman traces lacking. Atop the cliffs just inland from the Castle and Island, the Norman parish church of Tintagel in its churchyard overlaps some much older rectilinear earthwork that may be a Roman coastal signal-station. If a recognized route ended here it would explain why, of the five Roman milestones found in Cornwall, one (*c.* AD 308–24) was discovered in 1889 at the very entrance to the churchyard, and a second (*c.* AD 251–53) came from within a mile.

The excavated finds are not all post-Roman imports. Locally made pottery of the 3rd and 4th centuries AD, fragments of Roman coarse wares, and a 4th-century bowl from the Oxford region must be noted. Before the erosion of the slate neck had brought about the present near-island situation, Tintagel would have been a high, thumb-like promontory. On the landward side, cutting off such a promontory and providing it with an effective defence, a great ditch runs across the slope just outside the Castle. Enlarged in the Middle Ages, it may originally have been dug at some earlier period, since post-Roman pottery was found in the silt of the first-phase ditch.

All these observations fall into place. A native defended-promontory settlement, known in the area as 'the fort (*duro*) of the Cornovii', became in later Roman times a permanent or periodically manned administrative post, perhaps for the enforced gathering of taxes in the long north-Cornish coastal farming belt, perhaps (since it adjoins a landing-beach) for other duties akin to customs. As was usual, the Romans adopted the native place-name. That the site lay along an official route westwards across the Tamar is indicated by the later 3rd- and early 4th-century milestones, and by its inclusion in whatever route-sequence the Ravenna cosmographer subsequently used.

In post-Roman Dumnonia, Tintagel – under whatever name – would have had obvious attractions as a seat of power. Memories of an Imperial Roman function lingered. The place was naturally impressive. It was readily defensible, and possessed access by both land and sea. The ensuing Celtic establishment will have been a large one, since the relevant finds come from most parts of the site. The sheer quantity of imports, their exotic nature and far-flung origins, speak of a place where purchase was assured and a ready market was a matter of knowledge.

Why, then, the medieval castle – an elaborate and laborious construction in a place with no conceivable strategic importance, a white elephant among castles and one that, by 1400, was already starting to decay and to collapse? Oliver Padel's solution commends itself. Either Earl Reginald or the later Richard, preferably the latter, selected Tintagel simply because of its unique significance in the minds of his medieval Cornish subjects; not so much as to ingratiate himself in popular sentiment, as to exploit the belief in its once-royal tenure. So might a victorious Napoleon have set up shop in Windsor Castle, or the Tower of London. That belief (and, about the time of Earl Reginald, it was what Geoffrey of Monmouth encountered) peopled Tintagel with all the antique Dumnonian rulers: Gorlois, Mark, Cadwy, Tristan and the unknown rest. Note, however, that we have absolutely no warrant to think that Arthur was ever among their number. That notion was later, literary and of external origin.

Material culture

The remainder of our archaeological knowledge of post-Roman Dumnonia is, apart from the Christian remains (discussed last in this chapter), sketchy. External contact by sea during the 5th and 6th centuries is implied by a scatter of other sites yielding Mediterranean pottery. While there is no direct evidence for trade, and certainly no likelihood of *organized* trade on a large scale, there is also no reason to suppose that tin-streaming ceased when Roman Britain underwent administrative collapse. The cultural independence of mid- and west Cornwall is underlined by the continuation (rare in Celtic Britain) of native pottery-making, at first a range of jars and dishes which are later and slackly shaped versions of those used during Roman times, and after about 600 other types – flat-based pots, used for cooking directly over fires, whose bases bear chopped-grass impressions and whose rims are finger-crimped. These so closely resemble contemporary pottery from the north and northeast of Ireland as to suggest that actual Irish peasant-immigrants (arriving directly, or moving down from Irish-settled south Wales) were responsible for this quite new fashion.

39 Flat-based pots from northeast Ireland (*far left*) and west Cornwall (*left*), suggesting Irish immigration to Cornwall after about 600.

General exploitation of the countryside in a farming mode that will have combined cultivation of small enclosed fields with the raising of stock in larger pastures, common uncleared land and hill grazing proceeded apace between Roman and Norman times much in the way that it did in post-Roman Wales and parts of Ireland. The settlement unit, the farmer's actual home with outbuildings and the adjoined houses of relatives or labourers, was now unenclosed, and the place-name element *tre(f)*- emerges by the time of Domesday Book as the usual label. It does not mean 'hamlet' or 'village' in the southern English sense; Cornish dialect 'townplace' translates it, and 'agricultural holding' would be a technically correct description because a *tref* was clearly accepted as the homestead with ancillary buildings and all the land, a single social unit. One important Roman-derived innovation may have been an early mould-board plough, allowing the turning of a proper furrow slice. Actual traces of ploughing by such an implement were preserved, uniquely, in a sandy soil at the post-Roman site of Gwithian in west Cornwall.

40 Another Dumnonian chieftain-pillar (top later mutilated) from Stourton, Devon, the memorial of IURIUCUS, whose family have chosen to label him *Princeps* (detail of inscription, *near right*).

One's impression is nevertheless that of a peasant land (perhaps a slightly lop-sided impression, necessarily derived from Cornwall, where the evidence is more widespread than it is from adjoining Devon). Nothing approaching a town can be detected until shortly before Norman times, when there may have been a 10th-century fortified *burh* near Launceston. Some element of social stratification, the rise of independent farmers to make up a Dumnonian 'middle class', could be implied by selective use of inscribed memorial stones, and by the commemoration of early and prominent tenement-holders in place-names. Many names in *tre(f)*- are followed by male personal names, as they are in Wales. We looked at the evidence for Dumnonian rulers. A 6th-century stone at Stourton, west Devon, reads PRINCIPI IURIUCI AUDETI: if it commemorates *Iuriucus*, (son of) *Audetus*, the first word seems to be '(Stone of the) *Princeps*', and strictly this Latin word means 'prince', in the various senses of 'noble person', 'ruler', 'leader' (not necessarily a king's first son). Another stone, the so-called Men Scryfys or 'Written-Stone' in the Land's End peninsula, names a man called Rialobranus, involving earlier British *rigalo*-, 'kingly, royal'. Was he rather more than just a large landholder? If anything of the territorial muster-system implicit in the terminology of the Cornish hundreds belongs to Dumnonia after the Romans, we could look for persons with definite responsibilities for leadership – military or social – attached to districts. Most Saints' Lives are far too late as compilations to illustrate this, but the early 7th-century life of St Samson does introduce us to a crowd of north Cornish heathens within *pagus Tricurius*, the hundred later called Trigg, who have a very definite leader (*comes*, 'chieftain'), Guedianus. He stands in front of his followers, and later makes them all undergo baptism at the saint's hands. Conceivably the named persons, local rulers but clearly far less important than Dumnonian kings, who flit in and out of Cornish place-names, legends and medieval drama represent a class of minor territorial nobility.

Christianity

The Christian history and archaeology of the southwestern peninsula offers a particularly interesting field of study, because after a comparatively late start (end of the 5th century?) it can be followed, a few gaps apart, well into Norman times and the rise of the familiar medieval and modern system of parishes. Here again, at any rate in Cornwall, there is a kind of uniformity evenly spread. The Scandinavian disruptions found elsewhere (as in Ireland, Scotland and Northumbria) hardly occurred and, over five or six centuries, little local centres of Christianity grew up in their hundreds – perhaps (counting pre-Norman chapels alone) up to 600 or more. Most were simple burial-grounds for the Christian dead, ovoid or sub-circular embanked plots, to which the Cornish name-element *lann-* was usually attached (it had come to mean just 'enclosure'). The so-called developed aspect was the addition of a small chapel, and while by the 12th century some at least had been appropriated as the private chapelries of manors, it was from this plentiful and geographically well-distributed reservoir that about 150 chapels – some enlarged or rebuilt over the centuries, nearly all standing in burial-grounds – were selected to serve as the parish churches of the early Middle Ages. Even when the first small Norman churches had given way to longer naves, added aisles, and the high granite towers so familiar in Cornwall today, the clues as to Celtic, post-Roman Dumnonian, origins can remain in the form of the now much-raised circular graveyard; or, rarely, the lasting presence of an inscribed stone, memorial of a Celt whose remains have been in the same spot for fourteen centuries.

41 Granite in 12th-century Cornwall – a church-path cross with rounded head and simplified Crucifixion figure, Treslothan, Camborne. Contrary to popular belief, numerous such monuments throughout Cornwall are 12th or 13th century, not early Christian.

5·Early Scotland

HE LAND OF SCOTLAND is, in any detail, unknown to most Englishmen – just as it was to most Romans. From London to the eastern point of the Scottish border, at Berwick-on-Tweed, is about 300 miles; from Berwick to the northern tip of the Shetlands, in a direct line, is nearer 350 miles. Rome laid down Britannia's northern frontier twice, each time spanning an east-west constriction. Hadrian's Wall ran from the Solway to the Tyne, and the Antonine Wall from the Clyde to the Forth. It is a measure of the non-Romanization of North Britain that the more southerly, Hadrianic, frontier was the one eventually maintained and that the intervening Lowlands up to the Antonine Line, as a buffer zone, alone held those tribes with whom any kind of stable agreement was possible.

Well into the Middle Ages, the enormous northern region was as remote to all the remaining inhabitants of Britain as far Cathay or the distant Indies. Persons like Dr Samuel Johnson (shepherded by the native Boswell) were agreeably surprised to find a measure of domestic comfort in the Highlands and Isles. The Jacobite risings of 1715 and 1745, however, showed the dark side of the coin and revived fears dormant for a millennium. If Edinburgh had its own polite society and letters, the Highland tribes *en masse* were still – as they always had been – dangerous and possibly invincible. In London, Horace Walpole and his friends could shiver at the prospect of 'a fierce, desperate enemy, bold in imagined safety from the target [shield] and superiority of the broadsword'. When Charles Edward Stuart's fractious Celtic army reached as far south as Derby, 'the worst of miseries, slavery and superstition' confronted the Hanoverian southeast. John Wesley, visiting Newcastle in September 1745, vividly describes the terror, the drunkenness, the rioting and the dissolution of order as news came that the Pretender and his rebels had left Edinburgh; 'more and more of the gentry every hour rode southwards as fast as they could'. (Wesley found time to write to the Mayor of Newcastle, complaining of the open, flagrant wickedness and profaneness abounding in his streets.) So may it have been in Rome in 410, as Alaric and his fearsome Goths prepared for their final assault.

42 The 2nd-century Roman distance-slab from Bridgeness, Antonine Wall. A pictorial cliché, this nevertheless underlines the Roman view of Caledonian barbarians to the north.

Yet Scotland, within itself, was not for many centuries a single unitary nation or country. Edinburgh has been English-speaking since the mid-7th century. In the far northwest and the Isles where a Celtic speech (and attitude to life) lingers, the traditional rogue is not the poor Saxon, but the wily and rapacious Edinburgh banker or advocate. There are Orcadians and Shetlanders who recall their Norse background and can in all truth tell you that the nearest large railhead to Lerwick is not Inverness, but the slightly closer Bergen in Norway. The consciousness of this diversity, however expressed, lies in all Scottish literature and much of Scottish thinking – as it did even in Roman times, when the southern tribes knew others whom they called in their own language *Atecotti* ('The Very Old Ones'). When Alfred held the throne of Wessex, presaging the emergence of a full English nation, Scotland still contained (in uneasy combination) its Picts, Irish-descended Scoti, northern Britons and the first Norsemen. Celtic Scotland has to be approached through its early component peoples.

The Picts

The Classical names for both Britain and Ireland were mentioned in Chapter 2. Prehistoric Albion, maintained through Irish influence, became localized as a name for North Britain in the form of *Albu* (*Alba*, *Alban*). Its final remnants are the suspended Royal title, duke of Albany, and the Albany Heraldship of the Scottish heraldic Court of the Lord Lyon. In a sense, the Picts were also the Original Britons. The early Greek word *Prettania* implies that the Iron Age peoples called themselves *Pretani* or *Pritani*. Standing aside from the development of the more familiar Britannia, this much older version surfaces in late and post-Roman centuries (*Prydein*, the formal name for Britain in Welsh). And a related word, *Priteni*, was almost certainly a generic term for all the barbarians beyond the Antonine Wall. If we seek a meaning, the favoured view is that it arises from an older word implying 'people of the forms, shapes, or depictions' (*k^wrt-en-o-*). This would have been applied, by contemporaries, to those in the habit of tattooing or painting designs on exposed portions of themselves, and for the 1st century BC there is Caesar's notorious remark that 'all the Britons dye their bodies with woad, which produces a blue colour, and this gives them a more terrifying appearance in battle'. In the far north, something of this custom continued. By the 3rd century (and presumably, though we lack a dated record, considerably earlier) the Romans invented their own nickname *Picti*, 'Painted Ones'.

The mere fact that the Picts had a national name of Celtic origin, and that most of the recorded tribal names in North Britain are from the same stock, does not imply that they were universally Celtic; any more than the present inhabitants of 'Liberia' and 'Mauretania' are latter-day Romans. Even *les Français* – descendants of Romanized Gauls and the flag-bearers

43 The 18th-century English view of the wild Scots: portrait of Alastair Mhor Grant at Castle Grant, 1714.

of western civilization – owe their national label to their Germanic warrior neighbours, the Franks. The Picts are the most interesting, and least well defined, of all the peoples of Celtic Britain. With the advance of archaeological knowledge, studies become less speculative. Today, they allow the notion of an amalgam of tribes or groups, some harking back to the local Bronze Age and even late Neolithic, some having pushed northwards over five centuries or more during the Iron Age.

The distinction between the Picts and their various compatriots is both important and early. Between Hadrian's and the Antonine Wall, an influx of people from northern England (or further south) late in pre-Roman times would account for the view – probably also held by those Romans concerned with such matters – that the British here differed little from the native people actually *within* Britannia, inside the frontiers. Beyond them however lay total barbarism, a dark region suitable for campaigns and temporarily held coastal bases, but not really thinkable in terms of treaties with the natives or any kind of return on the capital required to assimilate the area into the Roman empire. Possibly (as on the Indian northwest frontier) wounded and abandoned legionaries fell on their swords, rather than be ritually dismembered and slowly roasted by the savages and their womenfolk. Tamed Picts would have been exhibited as natural wonders, like the occasional far-straying Eskimos in the late-medieval court circles of Scandinavia.

In fact the 'average' Pict, if he existed, given a 20th-century costume would pass without comment in the streets of Aberdeen; his principal concern was farming and stock-rearing. Settlements, scattered over the rich coastal plains of the northeast and along the valley floors among the picturesque Highland ranges, were not basically different from many in Northumbria, Wales and the southwest. Social and religious life would admittedly have had its own complexities and it is still not very clear how (or in how many ways) Picts disposed of their peaceful dead. The idea of this mixed ethnic background is reinforced by the existence into early historic times of two quite distinct Pictish languages. The non-Celtic one is known from a handful of very late inscriptions (samples: *irataddoerens . . . iddarrnonn vorenn ipuor*). All one can safely say is that, obliquely represented in late Ogham scraps (see Chapter 7), this language appears to have been non-Indo-European, and therefore comparable as a survival to the situation of Basque and a few other archaic tongues on Europe's periphery.

There has been an assumption, and this is all it can be, that Iron Age Celts entered Scotland after 500 BC; not so much conquering, as imposing their own rudimentary tribal structure where none had existed. In Roman and early historic times names of some (though not all) Pictish rulers are clearly Celtic, and so are the tribal names – *Caereni, Cornavii, Epidii* – and those of major rivers (*Deva* and *Tava*, the present Dee and Tay). The influence of a pre-Celtic majority may have been too strong and persistent to allow total change. In personal habits and custom, as perhaps in primitive religion, we can speak of a Pictish way of life. Early Irish and English writers knew few hard facts about the Picts, but they did know them as nationally distinct and socially peculiar. Bede – who was clearly interested in languages – not only regarded Celtic Pictish as distinct from Celtic British (which he knew slightly), but felt obliged to repeat a rambling story about the Picts arriving from 'Scythia' (Scandinavia?) with no womenfolk; wives were duly supplied by the Irish, on the condition that in cases of doubt Picts should elect their kings from the female royal line rather than the male. This underlines, if it hardly explains, the observation that Pictish succession *was* almost invariably through mothers; no king succeeded a father, though some succeeded brothers. Whatever principle was involved was non-Celtic. Isabel Henderson rightly thinks it highly probable the custom 'came from the native Bronze Age'.

We saw in earlier chapters how the British Celts, when the Romans encountered them, were grouped in tribes. It is still debatable exactly *how* the Picts were divided but the evidence suggests that, as a nation of perhaps a half-million people occupying an area much larger than Wales, divisions of a kind existed throughout historic times. The 2nd-century geographer Ptolemy, drawing his information from Agricola's Scottish campaign of AD 80 to 84, listed some thirteen peoples. Most if not all their

44 The tribes of North Britain (names from Ptolemy) in the early Roman period. With marginal exceptions all the names can be explained as Celtic. The tint shows land over 600 ft (c.180 m).

names would now be explained as Celtic, as also that of the Orkneys (Orcades, implying a tribal name *Orcoi* or *Orci*, 'Boar People'). Conversely, Ptolemy's *Ebudae* (the Hebrides or Western Isles) may be a rare instance of a non-Celtic name.

Of particular standing was one large tribe, the Caledonii. The associated area-name Caledonia was from Roman times often applied to all of Scotland north of the Forth-Clyde line and, poetically, is still sometimes used to mean Scotland itself. By late Roman times we find the Picts presented less as individuals and component tribes than as groupings. In the earlier 3rd century they were the *Maeatae* (nearer to the Wall) and the *Caledonii* beyond them; in 310, the *Calidones* and the 'other Picts'; and a half-century later, the *Dicalydones* and *Verturiones*. If the name *Maeatae* underlies that of Dumyat (Hill) in Stirling and the region of Fortrenn has its origins in *Verturiones*, it looks as if the division was basically between northern and southern Picts. There is no reason why Bede's remarks should not suggest a later form of internal grouping. Bede regarded the Picts as a nation (*natio*), but one inhabiting distinct provinces (*provinciae*), arranged in such a way as to permit him to talk about 'southern (*australes*) Picts' in contrast to Picts who were *transmontani* or *septentrionales*, 'across the mountains; western'. The great natural division is the mountain range running across Scotland from Aberdeen to Fort William, the Grampian massif, its eastern part being known as The Mounth. Much later (10th–12th-century) Scottish sources specified seven Pictish districts, explained as having been named after seven sons of a legendary Cruithne, or 'First Pict'. The district names are old and broadly identifiable and are mentioned in other sources, and by medieval times were regarded as one-time kingdoms. Great uncertainty must surround the whole matter but, viewing it cumulatively, the impression is that the Picts were tribal by the 1st century AD, and tended through geography to maintain a basic divide between their own North and South. It may also be said that, archaeologically, not all parts of Pictland shared quite the same material culture and that any such internal divisions may be marginally relevant to the development of Pictish art (Chapter 8).

The northern Britons

The Lowlands of Scotland, between Hadrian's Wall and the Antonine frontier, make up a great irregular rectangle some 120 miles east-west and 70 miles north-south, and a good third of the area is as mountainous and as unfavourable to early settlement as the Scottish Highlands. There is abundant evidence that during the whole Roman period this was the homeland of four tribes, whose cultural origins are linked with the later Iron Age of northeast England – the *Damnonii* around the Clyde Basin, the *Votadini* around the Forth, Lothian and the east-coast plain down towards Northumbria, and the *Novantae* in the southwestern plain of Galloway and Dumfries. The fourth (*Selgovae*) must be placed further within hill-country, in the upper Tweed basin; their name means 'Hunters' and, like the mysterious *Atecotti*, they may represent some degree of persistence of pre-Iron Age natives in the region.

These Britons shared the language, religion, and even place-name elements of their southern compatriots. In Kenneth Jackson's telling phrase, they spoke the same language that could be found all the way from Edinburgh to Penzance. While, for most of the Roman era, they lay beyond the northern defended frontier of Britannia, their territory from time to time contained Roman defensive settlements, and the extent of personal and commercial contact is implied by the large number of

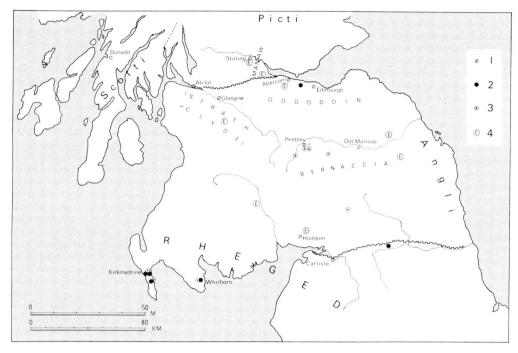

45 Sub-Roman southern Scotland and its initial Christian character. Symbols: 1 major Christian sites (note especially Whithorn and Kirkmadrine); 2, 3 inscribed memorial stones of 5th–6th and 6th–7th centuries respectively; 4 place-names in *Eccles-* (putatively early church sites). The names of kingdoms are in capital letters.

Roman coins and other small finds from native sites. Individual adventurers and bandit gangs apart, these British did not engage in sustained attacks on Hadrian's Wall or raids south of it, and it can be presumed that they themselves had a loose northern frontier with the far more aggressive, far less Romanized, Picti. Indeed, since the extent to which the inter-Walls British came to form a buffer zone of tamed natives remains a question of inference and interpretation, the suggestion has arisen that these tribes became *foederati* – bound by treaty to Rome and receiving advantages in return for peaceful behaviour and auxiliary defence. This may go too far. Although post-Roman sources suggest that native rulers claimed descent from figures with Roman names, we know that the Britons readily adopted such names and that, after the 4th century, this process was accelerated by Christianity.

The post-Roman native kingdoms here are of particular interest because the confines of geography allow us to see a degree of continuity. The Britons of Strathclyde, the area of the former Damnonii, remained more or less as an independent kingdom until the Anglo-Norman period. The Clyde headwaters formed the heart of this kingdom, with an ancestral stronghold at Dumbarton Rock on the north shore, and a

Christian centre (from not long after 500) at what is now Glasgow Cathedral. Curiously, despite its long existence and – in tenurial terms – its partial survival as the extent of the medieval bishopric of Glasgow, we know relatively little of this kingdom's history, beyond lists of the early ruling dynasty; we do not even know its Celtic British name, though an intelligent guess would be that it was some early form of the word 'Cumbria'. The northwest edge of Strathclyde is similarly obscure. Across the broad Clyde lay the first Scottish settlements, but Strathclyde probably went a little north of the old Antonine line, in the direction of Stirling to the ridge of the Campsie Fells and, taking in the later county of Dunbarton, up to the head of Loch Long.

On the other side of Scotland, the Votadini retained their name as the kingdom of Guotodin or (later) Gododdin. A major citadel comparable with Dumbarton Rock was Din Eidyn, presumably on the extremity of the great Castle Rock at Edinburgh and physically obliterated by the massive fortress of the present Edinburgh Castle. A subsidiary district or region, Manau, lay just beyond the Antonine line, around the Forth's headwaters and around yet another natural citadel at Stirling Castle. This – Bede's *urbs Giudi* – was important enough to provide one name for the Firth of Forth; *merin Iodeo*, 'the sea of Iudeu', in early Welsh.

It is unclear how far down the eastern coast the Gododdin kingdom extended, but probably rather less far than the earlier lands of the Votadini. During the 6th century, a tract from Berwick down to Newcastle – between the Tweed and the Tyne – saw conflict between the Britons and the invading (and eventually victorious) Angles of Northumbria. Since this became part of the Anglian Bernicia, it is tentatively identified with the preceding British Bernaccia, a short-lived native state separated from Gododdin by the mass of the Lammermuir Hills. It is more likely that Bernaccia arose, with Gododdin, out of older

46, 47 The northern Britons
(*Left*) *Altclut* or Dumbarton
Rock: natural fortress of the
Strathclyde British, on the north
bank of the Clyde near Glasgow.
(*Right*) Arthur's Seat: this extinct
volcano and traditional Arthurian
locality rises, dramatically, in the
heart of Scotland's capital.

Votadinian territory than that it necessarily represented a post-Roman kingdom of the Selgovae further inland.

The former Novantae in southwest Scotland, with the late-Roman Carveti in the Carlisle area and presumably a large portion of the Brigantian tribe or confederacy, appear in the 6th-century guise of the kingdom of Recet or Rheged. It has been suggested that two places at the extremities of this state, Dun*ragit* in Wigtonshire and *Roch*dale in Lancashire – they are, as a post-Roman crow would fly, a good 150 miles apart – contain the same place-name.

If the Picts' national attention was mainly turned towards their own affairs, and that of the Scots (below) to their ancestral Ireland, the Britons of southern Scotland appear to have acted and thought, not as prototype Scotsmen, but as the northerly population-element of England and Wales. There was a heroic age, a century or more of battles against Picts, Irish and Angles alike. Whatever circumstances gave rise to the body of 'Undying War-leader' tales that, in later Wales and Cornwall, centred upon the figure of Arthur, also occurred in North Britain. The region has its own Arthurian localities, headed by the dramatic extinct volcano in Edinburgh's Royal Park, Arthur's Seat. The pinnacle of heroic recital was reached in the long narrative poem known as the *Gododdin*, which describes the gradual gathering-together of Celtic leaders and their bands at Din Eidyn and then their march south to a disastrous battle against the Angles at Catraeth (Catterick Bridge, in Yorkshire). The date of the known recension is still hotly disputed, but the hard core of the poem, it is agreed, originated around 600.

By the 8th and 9th centuries, in the wake of the established English kingdoms and then the various Scandinavian raids and incursions, the physical separation of the North British from the Welsh and Cornish did not prevent some confusion in the field of heroic literature, poetry, genealogies and a British national mythology. Much that may properly have arisen in southern Scotland had become diffused and even re-located in Wales. The process was aided by the possession of a common language and protohistoric background, and by centuries of struggle against a common adversary.

Today, though one can readily find Highlanders and Aberdonians who are proud enough to be latter-day Picts – and even the odd claimant to Pictish royal descent! – it would be strange indeed to meet Lowland Scots who shared such emotions with regard to the Votadinians. The principal legacy of British times is to be found in place-names like Terregles, Penpont and Tranent. They mean nothing in the language of Robert Burns; but one finds them again in the sister dialect of faraway Cornwall (Treveglos, Penpons, Trenance). And it is amusing to notice that the antiquarian Sir John Clerk, Baron Clerk of Penicuik near Edinburgh – the origin of Sir Walter Scott's *Antiquary* – knew what 'Penicuik' once meant; he was in the habit of whimsically calling his home *Mons Cuculi*, Latin for 'Hill of the Cuckoo'.

The Scots

It has long been established that, from the late Roman period, Irish settlements occurred in western Britain; the explanation of such moves cannot yet be settled, but archaeology and place-name studies now lend increasing precision to the forms and dates of these colonies. Scotland was affected in more than one way. The distance between the Antrim coast and the Rinns of Galloway, the southwest 'finger' of Scotland, is a short one, and it is now possible to demonstrate a minor Irish movement into Galloway from the 6th century, extending thinly along the whole coastal plain to the river Nith. Since by the 8th century much of this area had fallen under the domination of Northumbrian Angles, the episode has left only specialized traces. The history of the major Irish settlement forms a very different matter.

It begins with a movement from Dalriada, approximately the coastal belt of the present county Antrim in Northern Ireland, across the intervening narrows to the west Scottish coast. The distances are short; from the northeastern tip of Ireland, only some 12 miles to the Mull of Kintyre, and 25 miles to Islay. This whole region of Scotland should, in Roman times, have formed part of the land of the Picts, and in early 8th-century Northumbria it was Bede's belief that Iona – and presumably therefore the island of Mull and the Argyllshire coastlands too – had in some fashion been ceded by the Picts to the Irish colonists. The traditional Irish founding-figure, Fergus Mor son of Erc, is not directly dated, but various calculations (and to some extent the evidence of archaeology) place the event at the end of the 5th century.

The Scottish settlement is depicted in the earliest sources as tripartite, each of the three regions being inhabited by a kin-group (*cenel*) named

48 Dunadd, on the Moss of Crinan: the principal citadel of the Dalriadic settlers.

after Loarn, Oengus or Gabran. The *Cenel nOengusa*, the least important, can be placed on Islay; the two major groupings, *Cenel Loairn* and *Cenel nGabrain*, lie respectively north and south of the long sea-inlet of Loch Fyne. It is important to realize both the proximity of western Scotland to northeast Ireland (the Dalriadic Scots continued to exercise a degree of rule over their original home territory for some time after the settlement), and the maritime element involved. Dr John Bannerman points out that in this region of long winding lochs, mountain ridges and scattered islands it was the sea, not the land, that unified so dispersed a colonization. The most important detailed source, Adomnan's late 7th-century life of (the late 6th-century) St Columba, records or implies at least fifty-five separate voyages, about half of them between Ireland and Scotland. Analysis of these, and other, early references points to composite craft, the ancestors of the Irish *curach*, of the hide-and-wicker kind of construction; normally propelled by oarsmen but able when necessary to raise a sail for greater propulsion. There is even a mention of a *bellum maritimum*, a naval engagement, between rival Dalriadic factions in 719 – as Bannerman rightly claims, the earliest recorded in native British history. It is a reminder that land-based archaeology, and indeed early history, can overlook this dimension of activity. Elsewhere Nora Chadwick drew attention – from Roman sources, Gildas, and certain native annals – to the currency among the Picts of what must have been similar craft, perhaps even camouflaged a sea-colour, for purposes of long-distance warfare.

49 Modern native Irish *curachs*, Blasket Islands, Co. Kerry.

Interaction

The history of Scotland, as a separate nation within Britain, conventionally begins about AD 841–43, when Kenneth mac Alpin, king of the (Irish-descended) Scots, became king of the Picts principally by conquest, rather less certainly aided by some claim to the Pictish kingship through his mother. Though this reign saw the two major components united, the resulting domain was much smaller than modern Scotland. It was not until the early 11th century that Malcolm II, defeating a Northumbrian army, finally acquired all of the eastern Lowlands down to the river Tweed. About the same period, on the death of Owen, king of the Britons of Strathclyde, this long-lived British realm was also absorbed when Malcolm's grandson Duncan assumed the vacant kingship. The precise frontier between Scotland and England remained for later definition. In the far north, though the Scottish king William the Lion subdued Caithness and Sutherland in the late 12th century, the Scandinavian Western Isles were added to Scotland by the Treaty of Perth (1266), and Orkney and Shetland were not obtained (Chapter 1) until the 15th century.

From the 6th to early 9th centuries, the story of Scotland north of the Forth-Clyde isthmus is not only too complex safely to be reduced to a short précis, but is also dependent on uneven and defective source-material. It would be misleading to depict it simply as the expansion of the Scots, at the expense of the declining Picts. The fact is that the Picts did not chronicle the events of their nation (and as far as we know were non-literate, until the stages when localized conversions to Christianity necessitated the use of Latin). It now seems fairly sure that a chronicle was maintained at a principal Scottish monastery, Iona, in the 7th (to mid-8th) century; it is less certain that, after that time, the Christian Picts could have produced a comparable level of record. Where events in Scotland are mentioned, they are mentioned in Irish compilations drawing upon Dalriadic material (or more general report), and they favour Scottish rather than Pictish activities.

Kingships, battles and deaths provide the skeleton or framework, and historians continue to add flesh to such bare bones. Scots, Picts and Strathclyde Britons figure here, battling from time to time in various combinations. The element of time, the necessary chronological scale, is provided by the dates assigned, progressively closer to the events in question through Irish sources, and then retrospectively in later and far more problematical Scottish ones. The zenith of Pictish dominance may not have arisen until around 600–650, by which period it is possible that the Picts controlled the Northern Isles and, on the west, the large island of Skye, beyond what is conventionally regarded as 'Pictland'. The prolonged survival of the insufficiently studied kingdom of Strathclyde is notable enough in itself; and on the corresponding eastern side of the

50 The citadel of Dunollie, crowned with a medieval keep; on the north side of Oban harbour, Argyll.

Lowlands, it is not always appreciated that the Northumbrian Angles' capture of the Lothians (including what is now Edinburgh) by the 630s implanted, permanently, a non-Celtic speech that in very much later times provided the medium for Robert Burns' immortal offerings.

Archaeology

The material culture – the catalogue of objects small and large used in agriculture, the home, crafts and warfare – does not lend itself to fine distinctions as between Picts, Scots and North Britons. The background itself was a general one, the common equipment of the 'Late' or non-Roman Iron Age of both Scotland and Ireland. Specific local or regional variations, attributable on grounds of history and geography to specific peoples, arise only in things like ornamental metalwork, here discussed in the chapter on Art. The archaeology of field monuments, larger sites and constructions, may be rather different, though here we are hampered again because of uneven knowledge. It is fortuitous, if annoying, that the Inventory survey volumes (of the Royal Commission on the Ancient and Historical Monuments of Scotland, or RCAHMS) do not yet extend to Aberdeenshire and Perthshire, the large counties that should hold most of the diagnostic field archaeology of the historic Picts.

Two particular topics, however, merit comment. Insofar as the written sources for early Scotland name locations as well as rulers, battles and events, they name fortresses, usually prefixed with the words *obsessio* ('siege' – presumably successful) or *combustio* ('the burning-down of' – presumably in the course of an attack). Such entries are richest in the period around 630–740 and a good half of the strongholds named can be matched confidently with known sites. Recently Professor Leslie Alcock's careful campaign, sampling through selective excavation the defences or the interiors of certain of the better-known citadels, shows that archaeology goes some way to confirm the findings. Dun Ollaigh (Dunollie) is a small citadel overlooking Oban harbour, a Dalriadic seat burned by enemies in 686 and 698, sacked in 701 and replaced by major re-fortification in 714. Seventh–eighth-century finds are appropriate to activity immediately next to the *dun* or fort, and a stout revetted rampart with massive blocks appears to be the 714 defences.

The same story can be told of contemporary Pictish and North British citadels. Those attributable to the Picts include Dundurn, near St Fillan's in Perthshire, for which a siege is recorded in 683. The summit citadel had a dry-stone wall with oak beams massively nailed or spiked together, which was destroyed by fire and then overlain by a second stone rampart. The range of radiocarbon results tends to confirm that this initial fortification was indeed the one destroyed in 683, and internally there were small finds relevant to the period. The stronghold of the Pictish king Bruide, visited by St Columba, is now generally identified as a site below the present Urquhart Castle on the northeast end of Loch Ness. Another citadel – Craig Phadrig – in the same area may have been a contemporary Pictish fort (re-occupied, though not re-furbished, between the 5th and 7th centuries on the evidence of finds and radiocarbon results). For the British, the central point of Strathclyde was Dumbarton Rock, a towering twin-peaked boss on the northern shore of the Clyde that Bede knew as Alcluith (*Alt Clut*, 'Rock of the Clyde') and described as *munitissima*, 'very strongly fortified'. The later 'Dumbarton' comes from a Gaelic name meaning 'fortress of the Britons'. Here, Alcock's excavations revealed a summit citadel with finds taking the occupation back into the 6th and late 5th centuries, and others proper to the recorded siege and capture of the Rock by two Irish Viking leaders in 870–71.

Some of these Scottish early historic sites have produced sherds of the imported Mediterranean pottery classes (A and B) discussed in Chapter 3. However, this is by no means all the dating evidence; there have also been fragments of Merovingian glass from contemporary northern France, small objects (knives, bone combs, certain types of pin or brooch and clay moulds for making the same) that possess a general date-value because they are also known from other, non-fortified, settlements in Scotland and Ireland, and pottery of two further groups, classes D and E.

Class D, a range of wheelmade grey bowls and mortaria (special bowls for food-preparation, of Roman origin), occurs at a few sites in southwest Britain and south Wales, and in Scotland at the defended sites of Mote of Mark (in Rheged) and Dunadd, on the Moss of Crinan in Argyll, probably the chief seat of one of the three original Dalriadic kin-groups, that of Loarn. Dunadd was captured from the Scots by a Pictish ruler in

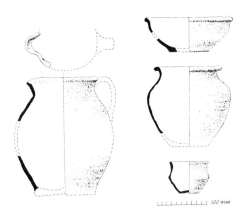

51, 52 **Class E imported pottery** (*Left*) The main types (handled pitcher, bowl, jar and beaker). (*Right*) Potsherds from Dunadd, Argyll, and Gwithian, Cornwall, showing the characteristic gritty stoneware surface of these imported domestic vessels.

736, has been excavated several times and appears to have been occupied since around 500. The class D material can be identified as a known Atlantic French product, 'Visigothic Grey ware', and its currency points to sea-borne trade. Class E is a more extensive range (pitchers, jars, bowls and beakers) of a dirty-white, yellowish, buff or orange pottery, not unlike a crude stoneware, and could be regarded as furnishing the equivalent of a kitchen – attached to an aristocratic household? – where foods were prepared in Roman-descended ways.

There is no doubt of the ultimate late Roman or late Gallo-Roman character of this material, or its large-scale production in some established manufactory. E ware occurs very widely all over western Britain and Ireland, and extends from the Isles of Scilly right up to Argyll and Skye. It has also been found on certain sites, mostly coastal, in Brittany and in the Channel Isles. Though the source remains unidentified, there is no reason to suppose that it lay within the British Isles. Somewhere in Atlantic France is far more likely, and what seems to be its Gallo-Roman precursor is now reported from Quimper, north of the Loire, and again in Bordeaux. The interesting point is that – along with D ware, and probably glass and some objects of metalwork – its importation must be separated from that of the Mediterranean pottery and also spans a longer period. Finds from Alcock's Scottish excavations, as from Richard Warner's at Clogher in Co. Tyrone, confirm the growing impression that, though class E may have been present in the southwest (Scilly, Cornwall, Devon) by the 6th century, the main phase of importation lay in the 7th, and even early 8th, century.

The European contacts implied by this take us back again to the question of external influences in the development of Christian monasticism. There are extremely limited historical allusions. The Irish, in both Latin and Irish-language sources, tended to stretch 'Gauls' and 'Gaulish' (Latin *Galli, gallicus*) to cover any non-Irish and non-British visitors, rather as in Egypt the words *firengi* (sing.), *afrang* (plur.) have for some centuries simply meant 'Europeans', though originally referring to Franks, or people on the northern side of the Mediterranean. Adomnan's Life of Columba notes a visit, presumably about 570–80, of *gallici nautae de Galliarum provinciis* – 'Gaulish sailors from the provinces of the Gauls' – to the chief place of the region, probably Dunadd. Irish Lives contain rather similar mention of 'merchants from the lands of the Gauls', etc. St Columbanus, a venturous figure from northern Ireland, found himself in the mouth of the Loire in 614 where a merchant ship was about to sail for Ireland. There must be a core of reality in all this, and the archaeological finds increasingly provide the material confirmation.

The remaining field archaeology of the various early peoples in Scotland is diverse, and where specific regional differences in house-types or modes of farming can be made out these are referrable in part to the underlying late Iron Age cultures. Peculiar mostly to Pictland are souterrains, or large semi-subterranean constructed passages – cellars, sunken byres, places of refuge? – attached to circular stone-walled houses, which began to be built during the Roman centuries but were used over quite a long period. In the Northern Isles (Orkney and Shetland) there is a complex archaeological phase before the Viking settlements of the later 8th century which must include, certainly in Orkney, the homes of Picts. Gradually, in the northeast Scottish coastal plain and the more fertile valleys, a picture emerges of mature farming landscapes, with settlements preferentially sited on the better soils. Again it has to be stressed that Scotland is a large country with difficult communications and that, while intensive fieldwork has taken place in a few small areas, there are plenty of bigger tracts where the full archaeological record will take years to compile.

Christianity

The conversion of Scotland to Christianity was piecemeal. The differing chronological horizons in the component regions are of some importance, because the advent of Christianity meant introductions both of external influences and of Christian literacy with its accompanying art and specialized archaeology. Unfortunately these horizons cannot yet be closely defined.

To the Britons between the Walls, the presence of 4th-century Christianity in Carlisle and sporadically among the Hadrianic garrisons with their civil settlements must have been apparent. It is on the western flank, along the coastal plain of Dumfries and Galloway, that tradition and archaeology combine to suggest the first implantation. The person known for many centuries as 'Ninian', a Briton whose Latinized name may have been *Niniavus*, remains shadowy but the context can be argued with some assurance.

Ninian first appears in the pages of Bede's *Historia*, in a short passage outlining the alleged antiquity of the conversion of the southern Picts. In this, he is by implication presented as a figure of late Roman Britain, a saintly bishop of the Britons who had been regularly instructed at Rome and who had chosen to ascribe his church and see to St Martin (of Tours, who died in 397). Explicitly, the church is located at somewhere called *Ad Candidam Casam* and it is described as having been built in stone – that is, a Roman structure and not the expected wooden church, and therefore built (as Bede comments) 'in a manner to which the Britons were not accustomed'. Bede adds that the place lies in a part of Northumbrian Bernicia 'which the English nation has just now taken over'. The English for *Ad Candidam Casam*, literally 'At the White House', is *Hwit-aern* or Whithorn, some distance west along the Galloway coast from Carlisle and the Solway. The Bernicians, who had extended westwards to Carlisle in the later 7th century, absorbed this long and fertile littoral in the decades before Bede completed his work in 731.

Bede, writing from the opposite side of Britain, could still have had easy contact with the new Bernician see at Whithorn and its first Northumbrian bishop, Pecthelm. Between the times of Ninian's putative foundation and the Anglians' arrival, this tract of southwest Scotland was subject to Irish settlement (including the probable foundation of an Irish-inspired monastery at Whithorn itself). Any later community of North British-plus-Irish clerics could have transmitted local traditions about the Founder – the antiquity of his church, the authenticity of his burial and shrine, and legends of his miracles – to their new spiritual rulers. Professor A. A. M. Duncan, however, now argues forcefully that one aspect of the Ninian tradition reached Bede quite independently. This is the southern Pictish claim that *their* conversion long ante-dated that of their northern compatriots, north of the 'steep and rugged mountain ridges'. In some fashion it went back to an episode 'when the word was preached to them by Nynia'. What kernels of truth are embedded in this, and what real dates are conceivably represented?

Here, archaeology has to take over. One likely explanation, perhaps the most likely, is that around 400, along the north shore of the Solway Firth and the Galloway coast, Romanized communities existed – either as descendants of the former Novantae, or as traders and fishermen hailing from Carlisle and a wider region south of Hadrian's Wall, or a mixture of the two. Whithorn, a sheltered township, is only just inland and still has its own tiny port at the Isle of Whithorn. Various Roman finds point to some such development. Around Whithorn there may have been a late 4th-century Christian community sizeable enough to warrant the provision of a bishop and the creation of a diocese. It would be perverse to suppose that any initial request would have been addressed further afield than to *Luguvalium*, Carlisle, the nearest episcopal seat. Niniavus, a priest, would have been elevated to a bishopric and sent in response.

53, 54 St Ninian and Whithorn
(*Right*) Preliminary indications of recent Scottish Development Department excavations in the modern town, by Peter Hill. The monastic vallum enclosure, with sherds of classes Bi and E imported pottery, should represent an Irish foundation later than Ninian and earlier than the Anglian occupation in the 7th century. (*Below*) The Isle of Whithorn – point of contact between the post-Roman settlement of Whithorn (just inland) and the Solway inlet with Carlisle. The end of the little double promontory has a small Iron Age fortification across it.

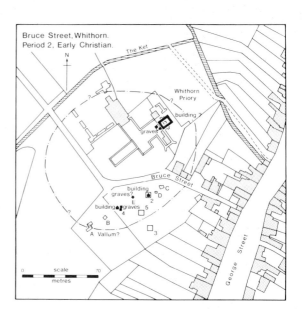

Bruce Street, Whithorn.
Period 2, Early Christian.

The inference is of some moment because, if anyone wants to look at it in this light, Ninian at Whithorn represents the dawn of Christianity within modern Scotland and it is wholly arguable that Ninian preceded both Palladius and Patrick in Ireland. His 'church of stone' may really have existed – a small congregational masonry church in a part-native mercantile settlement. The tiny ruin now visible, at a low level and protruding east from under the remains of Whithorn's medieval Priory church, cannot safely be presented (as it is, popularly) as Ninian's own. It is more likely to be a late 7th- or early 8th-century subsidiary church, an accretion to the founder's supposed grave and enshrinement and part of the pre-Anglian monastic development. Lastly, we know that post-War excavations deep below the chancel of the Priory went down through medieval burials, below the stone coffins of (?)8th- and 9th-century Northumbrian clerics, to simple oriented inhumation graves of Christian type that had themselves disturbed one or more cremations. This is an impressive sequence. It may mean that the nucleus below the subsequent churches was that of the first Christian burial-ground, itself perhaps sited where pre-conversion cremation burials were placed. If Ninian lay anywhere, it would have been just here.

How did this, putatively early, focus of Christianity affect the rest of southern Scotland? We grope in the dark. By the later 6th century, all the successor native kingdoms are presented as Christian; Rheged had Christian rulers and of course Whithorn, under whatever Cumbrian place-name, would have been one of several noted Christian centres within it. The Gododdin rulers, in Edinburgh and any other Lothian or Forth-region citadels, were Christians. The Strathclyde Britons had their own founder-bishop and saint, Kentigern (or 'Mungo', an abbreviated and affectionate form of the same name), and a focus equivalent to Whithorn lay below the present Glasgow Cathedral.

Some slight indication is given by the spread of inscribed memorial stones, together with their wordings and estimated dates. The centre of the see of Whithorn may, for a period after Ninian himself (probably in the later 5th and earlier 6th centuries), have been transposed to the next low peninsula westwards. Here, at Kirkmadrine, one such stone of *c*.500 or soon afterwards commemorates Viventius and Mavorius as *sancti et praecipui sacerdotes* (translated, preferably, as 'the holy and outstandingly excellent *bishops*'). Another, in similar style, names Florentius and a short name ending in -*s* (Iustus?). At Whithorn, a Christian family is commemorated – *Te Dominum Laudamus*, the stone proclaims, and then in devolved Roman capitals in horizontal lines we read that some person NEPUS BARROVADI ('grandson, or descendant, of Barrovadus') erected the memorial to Latinus aged thirty-five and his daughter aged five.

55, 56 **Early Christian Whithorn** (*Top right*) Early 6th-century bishops serving Whithorn? The Kirkmadrine inscribed stone, commemorating the *sacerdotes* (bishops) VIVENTIUS and MAVORIUS. (*Right*) Stone to Latinus at Whithorn, about AD 500 – perhaps representing three generations of Christian British.

The remaining inscribed stones south of the Forth-Clyde isthmus pad out the story, insofar as those dated to the later 6th and early 7th centuries are known from the Tweed valley and the southern shore of the Firth of Forth. They suggest a gradual spread of Christianization, mostly between 450 and 550, among the North British kingdoms. Of particular interest is Abercorn, now a small parish church not far west of Edinburgh. For a few years in the later 7th century, 681 to 685, it was the centre of a Northumbrian diocese, a bishopric created to serve the Christian Angles who since the 640s had occupied the Lothians. Our knowledge of Abercorn and its bishop, Trumwine, comes from Bede, and what he says is hard to puzzle out; but Trumwine's spiritual jurisdiction apparently extended *north* of the Firth of Forth, north of the line of the Antonine Wall that reached the Firth at *Penneltun*, the modern Kinneil. In this case it covered any Christian English who, following their king Oswiu's conquest of a southern province of the Picts in 658 – Fife may be meant here – had settled in what was geographically part of Pictland. The Picts recovered their territory in 685, after defeating the Northumbrian ruler Ecgfrith at *Nechtansmere* (Dunnichen Moss), expelling the Anglian settlers and causing Trumwine and his clerics to leave Abercorn.

None the less, in the tangled protohistory of North Britain, Abercorn retains the distinction of being the only place where the leaders of the Northumbrian church deliberately provided a bishop for Christians of three separate peoples – Angles, Picts, and any remaining Christian North Britons in Lothian. The arrangement that placed the episcopal seat in Lothian, Anglian territory, yet extended Trumwine's authority to a subject-province in the lands of the Picts – another, and eventually antagonistic, people altogether – is unique. St Patrick's 5th-century episcopate in Ireland was in no sense parallel.

Behind this lies the possibility (and it may be the basis of the traditions that Bede knew) that the most southerly of the Picts had been partially converted through contact with Christian Britons of the Gododdin kingdom. Though this is more likely to have been after rather than before 500, it was elaborated by Christian Picts into a claim that Ninian, the earliest appropriate bishop north of Hadrian's Wall, was ultimately responsible. That claim would have been meant to emphasize the distinction between Picts south of the Mounth, and the northern Picts whose conversion was admittedly later.

There are two, separate, traditions about the latter event, not necessarily conflicting, but in origin quite distinct. Bede himself, though he almost certainly never visited Pictland, knew people who would have done so. He met a delegation from the Pictish king Nechton which visited the Northumbrian monasteries of Wearmouth and Jarrow (Bede's home) in 710. These Picts, clerics among them, wished to be instructed in certain more regular observances and they also wanted skilled masons to help build them 'a stone church after the Roman fashion'. (The partly

57 Restenneth Priory church, Angus. The lower part of the tower, with its arched south doorway, represents an 8th-century porch built by Northumbrian masons after AD 710 for the converted Pictish king Nichtan.

8th-century tower at Restenneth, Angus, may reflect the Northumbrians' response.)

How, even by 710, could there have been Christian circles in Pictland, if only at the royal household? In addition to the claims involving Ninian and the southern Picts, the Pictish story – and this would have been given to Bede – was that the northern Picts had received the faith from the Irish settlers, the Dalriadic Scots. This does not mean that by 500 the Scoti were universally Christian, though we can assume that their settlements held Christian descendants of Patrick's northern Irish converts. It refers to the Pictish view that in 563 their king, Bruide son of Maelchon (ruler of all lands north of the Forth and Clyde), gave the small island of Iona to Columba, or Columcille, an Irish priest and abbot of aristocratic stock. The Picts (by Nechton's day, and as retailed by Bede) considered that Columba had crossed to Iona in order to convert those Picts who dwelled in the north, and that his mission – if later than Ninian's evangelization of their southern compatriots – was primarily Pictish in purpose.

58 Iona, the principal monastic centre for the Irish colonies in Scotland, where St Columba was first abbot.

Adomnan, ninth abbot in succession to Columba at Iona, wrote the founder's life around 690, nearly a century after Columba's death (597). Adomnan mentions journeys from Iona into Pictland,and at least one visit to Bruide's citadel, assumed to be in the area of Inverness. Elsewhere in the Life, a few Pictish families, among a nation depicted as overwhelmingly pagan, were converted and baptized. The Irish or Dalriadic view of Columba's life and work at Iona, which must be set against the Pictish version and which is what Adomnan gives us, implies that Iona, Mull and the Dalriadic Argyll region were already the lands of the Scoti, ceded by (or won from) the Picts in earlier times. The status of Iona emerges as that of the principal monastic centre for the Irish colonies, contact with the Picts being a secondary element.

The late Kathleen Hughes, in a penetrating analysis, concluded that it is not even clear that Columba converted and baptized the Pictish monarch, still less that he was in any sense a national evangelist. The (late 6th- and 7th-century) Columban foundations from Iona in Pictland were little more than 'minor cells, established without royal patronage, exercising little influence on society'. Had Columba's Pictish mission been rapidly and widely a success, rivalling the then-retrospective Irish inflation of Patrick's life-work; had he converted the Pictish king Bruide and his court; had he established churches and monasteries throughout Pictland in constant touch with the mother-house at Iona – then in 690 Adomnan would have said so. But he does not, and we must accept Dr Hughes' conclusions. Our first evidence that Christianity was a major influence in Pictish society comes after Adomnan's death (704), with the negotiations between King Nechton and the Northumbrian church. Nechton eventually chose to place Pictish Christianity alongside that of Northumbria, under the patronage of the Apostle Peter, and in 717 went so far as to send any Columban monks or clerics back to the Dalriadic kingdom.

Bede accurately reported what he knew, but his information did not reach sufficiently far backwards. In this case it came from a people who had almost no tradition of Latin literacy, an oral history in their own language or languages, and only their own interpretation of the past. The Picts cannot long have ceased to be pagan and in Bede's day it is doubtful that they were yet predominantly Christian. For example, it is very probable that certain Pictish forms of burial (long-cist burials, even cremations, in low cairns) which look superficially prehistoric are actually of the 7th or 8th centuries AD. Ninian, there is no reason to doubt, began the process of conversion among the North British in the 5th century and his successors reached some Picts in the 6th. Columba did likewise in the later 6th century among the northern Picts. From these beginnings, the process will have been much more gradual than has sometimes been supposed. In the case of the Picts, this conclusion has a direct bearing upon the nature and date of their distinctive art (Chapter 8).

6·Early Wales

F EW ENGLISH are taught the history of Wales in any detail. With the 120-mile land boundary separating, but at the same time physically joining, Wales and England it is remarkable that centuries of such contact have not brought about the disappearance of Welshness altogether. However, they have not; and one suspects that in certain ways Wales – the sunset-facing back room that John Bull so tolerantly and for so long has allowed his strange Celtic relatives to occupy – is actually experiencing an enhanced separation from the rest of Britain. If so, this is part of a greater centrifugal movement that future commentators can be left to describe.

The story of Wales from Roman times onward may be a prime instance of geographical determinism, more clearly perceptible in the 1st millennium AD than in later times. Communications show this well. Britain's (diminished) railway system is a case in point. Originally, from London two great routes went north, one aiming for Glasgow through the Birmingham–Manchester–Liverpool industrial heartland, the other through York and Newcastle up to Edinburgh and Aberdeen. By way of contrast, the main line to the South Wales ports, Cardiff and Swansea, was just an extension (through the Severn Tunnel) of I. K. Brunel's original and prestigious London-to-Bristol route. There *is* a line across mid-Wales to Aberystwyth, but only those who travel it will know how its builders had to cope with the obstacles of geography. An expert railway historian could chronicle the decline of the winding tracks, extreme north and extreme south, that used to serve the Welsh ports for Ireland – Holyhead and Fishguard. Air travel has virtually killed off these crossings.

It would be almost as hard for an English person to explain to (say) a Frenchman or Belgian the nature of the reciprocal attitudes between England and Wales, as it would be for a 100-per-cent Welshman to attempt this. Those attitudes, coloured by history at an extremely vulgar level, are almost invariably inaccurate. As depicted from central London, the Welsh sing; they mine coal; most of them are small and dark; they are Methodists who worship in box-like chapels with EBENEZER or PISGAH chiselled large, top front; their language contains many unpronounceable phonemes, and from time to time the essence of Welshness culminates in a secretive audio-visual display called *Eisteddfod*. Most of this is nonsense. Welsh choral traditions share with those of northern England, Cornwall and many parts of Ireland a late 18th-century Continental inspiration – still piously commemorated in Wales by the popularity of Haydn and Handel as baptismal names. The coal measures are confined to a small belt in South Wales and are hardly national in comparison with those of the English midlands and northeast. Average stature among the Welsh is probably the same as in England and Scotland, the only swarthy characteristic being an above-average incidence of dark hair. 'Methodism' in Wales shares its non-Anglican adherence with very large percentages of both Baptists and Congregationalists, and in any event is not Wesleyan but Calvinistic, a quite different church with its own late 18th-century Presbyterian structure. Anyone with a full set of teeth can learn to pronounce Welsh unvoiced *l* and *r* (the sounds written as *ll* and *rh*) in ten seconds flat: make the consonant sounds of H and L, or H and R, quickly and in those orders, expelling the breath sharply and disengaging the vocal chords. Eisteddfod – a label now frequently borrowed for music festivals elsewhere in Britain, if usually misspelled and invariably mispronounced – is a compound of two words cognate with 'seat' and 'abode'; originally it implied some kind of fixed ceremonial, Bardic, meeting-place and its current use stems from a conscious revival.

The Welsh view of England is not readily accessible. In the past it could tend to symbolize a peripheral discontent with distant power, or – making the most of what one has – to contrast rural virtue with urban squalor. Unfortunately a milestone in the expression of this tradition, the poetry of Dafydd ap Gwilym (*c.*1320–80; 'the earliest of the great singers of wild nature in medieval Europe') remains, in its native tongue, a closed book to English readership. Twentieth-century attitudes, when not verging towards caricature (as in the early Kingsley Amis novels, and most radio plays), might be illustrated from Arthur Machen's writings. In *The Secret Glory* (1923) the hero's father, an introspective mid-Wales scholar, has 'an oft-repeated exclamation, *cythrawl Sais*! (roughly = 'Saxon devil'). This 'damned not Englishmen *qua* Englishmen, but Anglo-Saxonism; the power of the creed that builds Manchester . . . that invents adulteration, suburbs, and the Public School system.'

The distinction between all this, and the contemporary southern British attitude to Scotland, needs little emphasis. But Wales has never been, as North Britain so often is, the playground of England's richer citizens; nor could the Welsh economy and society father all the political, legal and mercantile luminaries who, retaining their Scots origin, interpenetrate and frequently control the British establishment. As Prime Minister, Lloyd George was both an exception and a curiosity, and as such became rapidly embedded in folklore. Yet the English overlook the brilliance, and the genesis, of the House of Tudor. Queen Elizabeth I, standing in time and tradition somewhere between Boudicca and Queen Victoria, was with her red hair, exuberance, linguistic ability, stamina and devious skills a quintessential Welsh heroine.

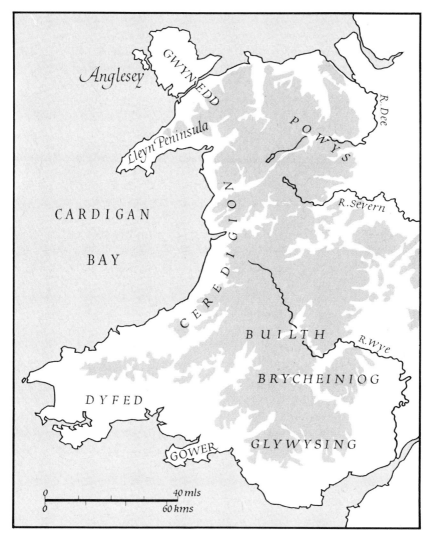

59 Known kingdoms of early Wales. The tint indicates land above 600 ft (*c*.180 m) and shows how geography has always forced major habitation to the rim of the country.

English A B C D E F G H I J K L M N O P Q R S T U V W X Y Z

Welsh A B C CH D E F FF G H I L LL M N O P R RH S T U W Y

Irish A B C D E F G H I L M N O P R S T U

Modern dictionary alphabets in English and the two main Celtic languages. In Welsh spelling CH, LL and RH are separate aspirated consonants, F and FF represent English V and F, and W and Y are primarily vowel-sounds. Irish also has aspirated consonants, but these are not distinguished alphabetically.

Wales remains, then, unexpungeable; as enigmatic and perhaps as faintly hostile to most non-Welsh Britons as it was in the Middle Ages. Those unlucky enough to arrive by car late at night in some unfamiliar Welsh town, only to find all the street-signs defaced or removed, should reflect that – as with everything else about Wales – the simple explanation is almost certainly the wrong one. The activity in question is not necessarily anti-English (or not more so than any other anti-Government protest anywhere). It is as likely to represent dissatisfaction with a local authority's policy, or even disagreement with the official Welsh version of Station Road or Jubilee Street, right down to such details as the insertion or omission of a circumflex accent on selected vowels. Purism is at stake, and will be defended by (rival) guardians of a tongue that took shape in the late pre-Roman Iron Age. We sense the existence of a world, within that larger looser world of Britain, stolidly upheld in the age of the microchip and the nuclear reactor. Is it possible to explain, even to sketch, in one short chapter the historico-geographical circumstances that led to the emergence of Wales as an entity?

The emergence of Wales

Wales, as relief maps show at once, is made up mainly of land over 600 ft (c.180 m). A region of great geological interest, its physical characteristics, pattern of soil-types and incidence of high rainfall do not make it an agrarian paradise. Much of Wales is still as 'wild' as when George Borrow visited it in the 19th century. Old tracks became lanes and those lanes have now been metalled into roads, so that few parts outside the mountain-blocks are truly inaccessible to vehicles but, as with Scotland, we must take care not to project contemporary land-use into remoter pasts.

The Roman conquest might appear, again from any reliable map of this, to have been no more than partial. It was sufficient. Wales, in area about one-sixth that of England, has a population now only a seventeenth of the English total. In Roman times, following the most cautious guess, it may have been 200,000 at the outside, with concentrations around the coastal plains and a scatter, inland, of hamlets and herdsmen.

In the division of Britannia, Wales eventually formed the great western half of Britannia Prima (centre, probably Corinium or Cirencester). The road-pattern of the Romans has all the appearance of a mountainous frontier province being served by military arteries. Gateways to Wales, north and south, were the legionary fortresses at Deva (Chester), and at Isca (Caerleon on Usk), backed up by the fortress and later *colonia* at Glevum (Gloucester). The less urgent centre was guarded by Viroconium (Wroxeter), west of Shrewsbury, itself still the hub of entry to mid-Wales. The northern route led to the fort at Segontium by the modern Caernarvon, whence vulnerable Anglesey – last stronghold of the Druids, so picturesquely and early reduced by Suetonius Paulinus and then Agricola – could be watched and the north Irish Sea patrolled. The southern route, which supported a further network inland, went to Moridunum ('Fortress by the Sea') at modern Carmarthen. The whole toponymy is redolent of initial conquest and fortification; Latin *castrum*, later Welsh *caer*. An economic historian might interpret the Roman communications system – its positioning, extension and density – in terms of which parts were actually inhabited at all; there would be no point in subduing unoccupied hill-country. Desirable economic resources typical of the highland zone were another factor: copper and lead on the north coast and Anglesey, numerous potential quarries, some iron on the southern approach (Monmouth, Glamorgan) and the famous gold-mines at Dolaucothi, 'the Old Pits', in Carmarthenshire.

When, as we believe in the 5th century, the first native principalities took form, one senses a very limited harking-back to pre-Roman Celtdom. At the level of individual dynasties, genealogies constructed later in the 1st millennium preferred to introduce great Roman founder-figures like Magnus Maximus and Constantine I. Of the principal tribal groupings reported in early Roman sources, only the Demetae in the far southwest handed their name to a native state (Demetia, Dyfed); others, if commemorated at all today, are geological adjectives like 'Ordovician'. Among the recognized tribal centres or cantonal capitals, Venta Silurum became Caer*went*, Moridunum Car*marthen*. Where urban centres in any shape or guise – road-junctions, early monastic settings, salvageable buildings, perhaps even part-defended enclosures – had a role to play in post-Roman life, then the Romano-Celtic names allotted by Rome to all such (non-Celtic) creations were perpetuated as often as not. So *Gobannium*, 'place of the blacksmiths', gave rise to Abergavenny (strictly 'Mouth of the Blacksmiths' River'). Neath started as a fort named *Nidum* and, west of it, fort called *Leucarum* is probably today's Loughor.

Our detailed picture of Celtic Wales, 400 to 700, remains sadly defective. We know a few defensive sites, excavated and yielding imported pottery like Dinas Powys (Glamorgan) and Dinas Emrys (Caernarvonshire), but not enough have been examined to confirm that they typify all chieftainly strongholds. Some Roman establishments were re-used – the shore-fort at Caergybi, for an early monastic church. Peasant homes and hamlets *may* belong to this era but frequently an excavation yields no datable finds. Any documentation identifying specific sites tends to be late and unreliable. Yet it is fair to add that field survey can and does enlarge this vista, either working forward from known Roman-period land use or backwards from securely dated medieval tenures. Pottery, rightly supposed to be the main prop of archaeological dating of excavated sites, was hardly made at all in Wales after the Roman period. In the transition from a sparse and agrarian Roman fiefdom to a mosaic of post-Roman Celtic kingdoms, it may have to be accepted that conventional archaeology is a poor guide.

60, 61 **Dinas Emrys: native citadel**
(*Right*) View of the ruined ramparts.
(*Below*) Mediterranean imports: reconstructed
pottery roundel (part of a lamp) found at the
site, with Christian ornament, 4th–6th centuries;
and a Phocaean Red Slip ware dish, early 6th
century, from Dinas Powys.

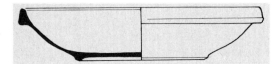

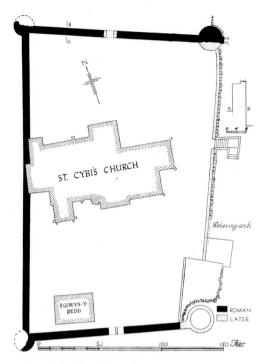

62, 63 **Church and homestead**
(*Left*) Plan of the late Roman
shore-fort at Caergybi, Anglesey,
a medieval church within its walls
– traditionally a Christian
monastic foundation granted to St
Cybi by King Maelgwn
(Maglocunus) of Gwynedd in the
6th century. (*Right*) A peasant's
hut at Din Lligwy, Anglesey,
occupied in Roman times.

It may also be a mistake to look for a separate, distinctive, post-Roman archaeology. Patterns of British settlement at this date were probably common to Wales, the Welsh border and the West Midlands. Apart from any 'upland' and 'lowland' distinctions of physical geography, there was no actual frontier until Offa's Dyke was constructed in the late 8th century. It cut off Wales from Saxon England, a massive symbol; though from the dark lands behind it, until well past the time of the Tudors, strange drovers could urge their beef on the hoof across to England's midland markets, to be grudgingly served refreshments at pubs like *The Welsh Pony* in Oxford. But Offa's extraordinary linear earthwork of the 780s, outcome of this Mercian king's political ambitions, is far less relevant to the shaping of early Wales than two other, previous, happenings.

The westwards drive of the Northumbrian Angles, in this case from their southern (Yorkshire) realm of Deira, reached the Dee when King Aethelfrith 'led his army to Chester and there killed a countless number of Britons' (613 or 616). Bede, who much expands the bare Chronicle record, saw the punishment of contumacious Celts in what was undoubtedly a major defeat for them. Slightly before this (577) Ceawlin and Cutha with the war-host of Saxon Wessex fought the British at Dyrham, just north of Bath and where the western rim of the Cotswolds falls into the Severn floodplain. Three kings were slain, and the English captured Gloucester, Cirencester and Bath, perhaps these monarchs' respective seats.

The English victories at Chester and Dyrham are so frequently cited that, as Professor Wendy Davies remarks, they have become historical clichés. The consequent English advances are depicted as broad wedges reaching the Atlantic coast at the Chester Dee and the Severn estuary, cutting off Wales and the Welsh Britons from all their compatriots north (Lancashire and Cumbria, the Lake District) and south (Somerset to Cornwall). The victories and advances happened. Their broad reality can lead to a map entitled 'The Isolation of Wales, *c*. AD 600'. Linguists agree that the separation of Late British dialects into the Cumbric, Welsh and Cornish languages followed. But in the early centuries, between England and Wales as now defined there was no clear-cut political or linguistic watershed. For example, Christianity was not implanted deep within Wales by missionaries from afar. Pretty clearly it had moved westwards from late Roman Christianity, and the whole British Church, implicit in Bede and earlier sources, was a Christian sphere linking the relevant areas of Wales and much of western Britain. The Welsh Border was, historically, not a frontier but a region of great significance. Our best index of a sub-Roman ruler's centre comes from Wroxeter where Philip Barker's meticulous campaign at Viroconium has uncovered, within that extensive part-military, part-civil tribal capital of the former Cornovii, a sub-Roman continuation. Grandiose in conception almost to the point of being labelled neo-Classical, this massive hall with its linear spread of outbuildings and even shops(?) was executed in timber, not stone. One could hazard the guess that ancestors of a 6th–7th century petty king, Cynddylan, founded their line here. And again we should note what happened to place-names. The Wrekin (earlier, in Welsh, *Guricon*, *Urecon*) is just Viroconium. Down in Herefordshire, Ariconium, a Roman settlement at Weston-under-Penyard, spawned names for the early Welsh district of Ergyng and the English *Archen*(field). Nor must it be forgotten how plenteous are purely Welsh place-names east of Offa's Dyke, or that Welsh could still be heard well inside these English marcher counties up to the Civil War in the 17th century.

But – absolute dates apart – one irrelevance of Chester, Dyrham and the Dyke resides in the chance that we may be induced to look the wrong way. 'Fog in Channel: Continent Cut Off' was a favourite headline in Edward VII's reign. Sub-Roman Wales was instantly open to Ireland and, in its story, the Irish dimension was of much importance. Leaving aside the incidence of late Roman trade involving any part of south Wales with the south and east of Ireland, there was actual Irish settlement; there are problems in dating its commencement (from diagnostic finds, or by reckoning backwards through later genealogies), but it may have begun before 400.

In northwest Wales, opposite Leinster, the Llyn peninsula – the long 'pig's ear' – may in its name contain Irish *Laigin*, 'Leinstermen'. Sporadic incursions of families and small bands, assimilated as farmers and pastoralists, could be one aspect of a much larger North Irish Sea movement. This took the Dalriadic Scoti to Argyll, other Ulster folk across the narrows to Galloway and (less known) Irishmen to the Isle of Man. Here, as far as can be detected, the speech of a surviving British population was replaced by the Irish ancestor of Manx well before the Viking age. In southwest Wales from Pembroke to the Gower peninsula, intensity of settlement was greater. In remembering this, both Irish and Welsh sources portrayed it as a tribal migration of the Irish Déssi or Déisi headed by their own king and, from the Irish viewpoint, a suitable 'expulsion' saga was adduced. The direct line of Irish rulers of Welsh Dyfed went on into the 7th and 8th centuries. An interesting mix arose; by 400 Irish and British were fully differing languages, and additionally Christians from both nations used different scripts (Latin and Ogham) for their memorials. Irish never replaced British in Wales the way it did in Scotland, but relative numerical strengths do not necessarily explain why; less obvious factors could be involved.

In Pembroke, Carmarthen and southern Cardigan, did Irish pastoralists extend former land-use and modify stockbreeding traditions? The late Professor Melville Richards plotted the distribution of *cnwc*, 'little hill, hillock', as a borrowing from Irish *cnoc*, to show close correspondence with Irish settlement in Dyfed. He also noted the retention in that area of a dialect word *meidir*, *moydir* – 'lane, farm-road' –

64–66 **The Irish dimension** (*Above left*) A purely 'Roman-inspired' stone from Penmacho, Caernarvonshire, with its horizontal lines of capitals and the neat chi-rho: 'Carausius lies here, in this heap of stones.' (*Centre*) Compare the vertically set 6th-century inscription from Henllan Amgoed, Carmarthenshire, to Quenuendanus, son of Barcunus – Irish names, repeated in Ogham symbols up one corner of the slab. (*Above right*) Place-name elements indicating Irish settlement in Wales (dialect words for 'lane') and Scotland ('mountain').

as another early loan. Irish *bothar* today means simply 'road', but its 1st-millennium ancestor had the narrower sense of 'cow-going; passage for cattle'. To reinforce this, in another area of minor Irish colonization, mid- and west Cornwall, the corresponding term in Cornish (*bounder*) may partly share this origin, at a post-Roman stage where settlement archaeology suggests that much wooded countryside was being opened for mixed farming.

In Wales there is also a considerable spread of memorial stones pointing to Irish settlement, and influences. The incidence of Oghams (highest in Pembroke) is a crude guide, and better is the contrast between the sub-Roman tradition of Latin text set horizontally and the use of HIC IACIT ('here lies'), and the reflex of Irish tradition with any inscription set vertically and the formula A FILI B ('of A, of the son of B'). This latter imitates the more 'Celtic' phrase peculiar to Irish Oghams (A MAQQI B). We are in the 6th and early 7th, rather than 5th, centuries. From the pattern of these memorials, from the postulated originals of lives of

Welsh saints collated in medieval Latin and from very close study of place-names, it is possible to define the emergence of Christian Wales; the details of individual religious foundations, be they monasteries or cemetery-churches, have to be supplied archaeologically. Our history is silent about survivals, if any, of pre-Christian cults, but there can be no doubt that around 600 Christianity was the prevalent faith.

The emergence of the oldest Welsh kingdoms is no easier to define because, as Wendy Davies now shows, one must separate all references to kingdoms as such that omit any names of the contemporary kings; references to rulers and their lines, normally constructed very much later as genealogies and regnal lists, that may be devoid of the relevant principalities; and lastly references to regions and territories within Wales, perhaps of great age, that did not necessarily ever rank as kingdoms. When Gildas wrote some time after 500, addressing five kings, the names of their kingdoms were incidental, but what he says is evidence for Venedotia (Gwynedd, the northwest) and Demetia (Dyfed, the Irish-dominated southwest). Dumnonia of course lies outside Wales, being Cornwall, Devon and part of Somerset. It can be argued that a fourth monarch, Cuneglasus, ruled between Gwynedd and Dyfed and it could be guessed – no more – that he was king of Ceredigion, the long coastal fringe of Cardigan Bay. The fifth king, Aurelius Caninus, might be linked with the southeast and its legacy of Romanization, the early Glywysing (or roughly Monmouth and Glamorgan). The kingdom of Powys spanning the northern Welsh Marches curiously derived its name from descriptive Latin, not Welsh (*pagenses*: '(land of the) country-dwellers', or 'people of the *pagi*', the Romans' equivalents of district-council areas). And alongside these larger entities, their names at last familiar throughout Britain since they were revived after 1974 as local-government regions and postal addresses, there is some evidence of smaller kingdoms and principalities. Some, like Brycheiniog and Meirionydd, are fixed because they supplied names to medieval shire counties on the English model (Brecknock or Brecon; Merionethshire). Others, like Builth and Gower, are known now only as towns or minor features (Builth Wells, the Gower peninsula).

Earlier it was suggested that Anglo-Saxon advances to the Dee and Severn might be exaggerated in talking about an isolation of Wales. Nora Chadwick reminded us that the natural route between the northern British – Cumbria, the kingdom of Rheged and the Scottish borders – and Wales was by sea, and a boat-trip down the coast from the Solway avoided the many wide river mouths and marshes of the Lancashire shore. The link was apparently both close and prolonged. In recent decades it has been realized that a great body of tradition, housed in Wales later in the millennium and expressed in Welsh poetry, heroic literature, pseudo-history and annals, may be truly British but still in large part Northern, not originally Welsh.

67 Offa's Dyke near Llanfair Waterdine, Shropshire.

One motif deals with the countering of Irish settlers, even to the point of expelling them; were it taken literally it would be at odds both with accepted chronologies and with what can be inferred in other ways. There is the story of Cunedag or Cunedda, ruler of Manau Guotodin (a district around Stirling, implicitly within the southeast Scottish kingdom of the former Votadini), induced to migrate with eight sons and one grandson all the way to northwest Wales, where they drove out the Irish and where the various descendants gave their names to the Welsh kingdoms and founded the kingly lines. Much discussion has ranged over the likely date, four generations before the 6th-century king Maelgwn of Gwynedd, with the corollary belief that this was a piece of final Roman or sub-Roman *Volkspolitik* arranged by some suitably powerful authority. Few scholars now suppose this ever happened, or happened on anything like the scale depicted. But the transfer of so much of British tradition – of kings and battles, bards and magicians – from Gwyr Gogled, 'the People of the North', to still-British Wales as the Northumbrians and Scots made inroads upon the former, brought to the principalities (and indeed, faintly, to distant Cornwall) a shared past. Within it, the disentangling and the arguments towards any original localities and persons must continue. There are suspicions that the hero Arthur and the sage Myrddin (Merlin) were North British and had little or no connection with their myriad traditional sites in Wales or the southwest. When in the 9th–10th centuries the native historians put together what they could find of times past, that of British Wales was not fully distinguishable from British Cumbria.

The later story of Wales involves slow moves towards central kingship and relations with the Anglo-Saxon rather than Viking and Irish worlds. Defective the picture of early centuries may be, but one of a mosaic of smallish kingdoms mostly lying around the central upland bloc is indicated. Owing much at technological, agricultural and linguistic levels to the Iron Age Celtic past, and with a less definite and geographically patchy indebtedness to a Roman occupation that involved but never radically altered the country, Wales remains to be explored in a dozen ways. Celtic Wales, in the sense of the period 400 to 700, emerges with just sufficient lineaments to reveal a part of Old Britain with characteristics we can only call, already, quintessentially Welsh. All its subsequent history has to be understood in that light.

Voyagers overseas

In stressing the role of early colonists in Wales we might also think of the unusual part played as colonists by the Welsh themselves. A medieval legend told how Madoc, a North Wales prince, discovered America and returned with his followers to the New World; from the 18th century, tales of Welsh-speaking Indians were circulating. America promised a haven where, remote from English sectarian, linguistic and political oppression, Utopians might create a New Wales. Individuals journeyed to search for Madoc's mysterious Indians, the Lost Brothers. The settlement of Beula, a mile square, was founded within elaborate and complex ideals in Pennsylvania and proclaimed as a national home for the Welsh on Bastille Day, 1795. It did not last. Even more strange was the second establishment of a Gwladfa (neo-Welsh for the concept, *gwlad*, 'country, homeland', *-ma*, 'place, spatial extension') by Michael Jones during the 1860s in Patagonia, part of Argentina. Farms were laid out, chapels built, literature printed and Welsh values upheld and taught. Here, Welsh-English bilingualism gave way to Welsh-Spanish, to the degree that later descendants might piously visit Swansea or Cardiff and fail to be understood. The dark side of the tragi-comic history – and, in Gwyn Williams's words, the initial dreams and labours were on a heroic scale – was seen in the Falklands struggle of 1982. For all one knows, Miguel Williams from Y Wladfa, enlisted to recapture Las Malvinas, would have been exchanging lethal fire with Michael Williams of the Welsh Guards. In no other way, however, can the intense devotions accorded by the Welsh to their own abstract and ideal realization of Wales be more poignantly demonstrated than through such New World quests. Not all colonies have to be the outcome of simple land-hunger or direct expulsion by a neighbour's aggressive conquest.

As for present Wales, is it (as patently as larger Scotland, or freestanding Ireland) the end-product of its early history or a different country altogether? The contention that Welsh nationhood is still in process of formation and that it took England's neglect to bring this about is one that many would take seriously. Wales is different and stereotypes continue. It remains a country where music is highly valued; the Welsh National Opera is so good that it should have been founded years ago, not recently. When Welsh teams visit Cornwall, another area where 'football' means *Rugby* football, it is assumed that their matches constitute the real thing, not the kind of match one might see in Kent or Essex. A diversity within Wales itself is detectable (geographical determinism again). Factually there are differences between spoken Welsh, north and south, notably in certain vowel-sounds too outré for English mouths to manage. Folk-belief houses the odd idea that North Walians are tall and gloomy Hell-fire chapelgoers who dislike visitors, those from the south being shorter, burlier and much more amusing. The true state of the Welsh language – away from its militant upholders – is hard to deduce from official returns, but it is patently not true that revived bilingual education stultifies the young mind, any more than it has done in Switzerland, Israel or Iceland.

7·Church and Monastery

THE TRAVELLER in Celtic Britain today, especially in Wales or Cornwall, who likes to visit old churches may be conscious of a past not quite the same as that he would detect in Essex or Sussex or Wiltshire. Admittedly the parish churches, if they do exhibit that air of medieval solidarity coming from massive granite building-stones and chunky towers, lack the soaring grace of so many classically English ones – the structures that attracted the brushes of Turner, Constable, John Sell Cotman and John Piper. But it is the village or parish names that imply peculiarly 'Celtic' circumstances. About a third of Cornwall's parish-church villages and small towns are still called 'Saint' Something or, if this prefix has been dropped, are still named for obscure saintly patrons: Gunwalloe, Zennor, Kew and Endellion. Any guide-book in Wales will tell you that *Llan-* means 'Church of', and a place called Llanaelhaearn therefore began as a settlement around a church with a patron, presumably called *Aelhaearn*. Clearly we are in a different league altogether from a pleasant English countryside where churches bear dedications to Saints John or Andrew or Paul, to the Blessed Virgin Mary, or to All Saints. And worse is to come. A nice outing around Anglesey in north Wales, the island jewel of modern Gwynedd, may include a halt at Llansadwrn. The church was re-built in 1881; but go inside, and observe in the wall of the chancel a small slab with Roman capitals. It reads (supplying the rest of a few words trimmed off) HIC BEATUS SATURNINUS SEPULTUS IACIT ET SUA SANCTA CONIUX PAX VOBISCUM SIT. Obviously this was an old tombstone. What it says is: 'Here lies buried blessed Saturninus and his saintly wife. Peace be with you both.' Again, a reliable guide-book will give the agreed estimate of its date. This tombstone was first carved and set up, marking the grave of a Christian Venedotian and his spouse, somewhere around AD 530.

Here the penny should drop, and into the correct slot: is the name Saturninus anything to do with the name following Llan- in Llansadwrn? Why not? Historians have long assumed as much, and Sadwrn is known to have been the brother of a very famous early Welsh saint, Illtyd, who may have died between 527 and 537. Does this mean that a church has

68, 69 **Christian continuity** (*Above*) Latin tombstone of Saturninus, 6th century, at Llansadwrn church, Anglesey. (*Below*) St Alban's, a major centre of British Christianity. The late Roman inhumation cemetery, presumably attracted to the burial and shrine of the 3rd-century martyr Albanus himself, is on the south side of the nave of the medieval abbey.

stood here for fourteen-and-a-half centuries, the interval between the Crucifixion and Columbus's discovery of America? Not necessarily; for the term *Llan-* began by signifying a burial enclosure, then a cemetery with a church, then the church itself and now any superimposed town (like Llandudno); but it certainly implies a continuous Christian locality, and plenty of others may be encountered.

There are sequences nearly as impressive in Saxon England, where the older cathedrals, like Winchester, are (with extensive rebuildings) the centres of 7th- and 8th-century Christianity. Their foundations, their first bishops and saints, and ancillary details, were described by Bede and many later writers. St Alban's, some 20 miles north of London, is (exceptionally) a 4th-century foundation, growing from the burial and shrine of Albanus, Britannia's own first martyr. If then we take, on the one hand, the considerable body of evidence for Christianity in the last century of Roman Britain and, on the other, the 6th-century Christian world – exemplified by Saturninus and Llansadwrn – in Wales, Cornwall, southern Scotland and Ireland, what is the connection?

Celtic Britain, when described at all by its internal sources (Chapter 2) or less commonly from contemporary Europe, is depicted as overlain by Christianity. Gildas's five kings are Christian and his muddled world is harangued, not for any lack of bishops and clerics, but for the pastoral shortcomings of those men. Ireland's own Christianity dates officially from AD 432 (Patrick's arrival; see below) and the supposed date of Patrick's death in 461 was marked in 1961 by that most significant of national symbols – an issue of commemorative stamps. St Alban has yet to enrich philately in Britain.

For Celtic Britain, as opposed to Ireland, there have been conflicting explanations, which persist and have to be mentioned. One view is that Roman Christianity, virtually confined to town life in the south and east, perished along with urban order and Roman ways after about 425–50. If at a subsequent date the Faith is manifested in regions north and west, beyond the early English settlements, then it may have been re-kindled from other and still-Christian provinces of the western empire, a fresh evangelization from overseas (the 'Gaulish missionaries' hypothesis). Another suggestion is that, allowing some such contact, Christianity was diffused northward and westward during the 5th century to regions where it had been scarcely known, through well-to-do Christian refugees fleeing in the face of Saxon advances and internal strife. Coupled to that is the wider hypothesis in which the Romanized British, natives of Britannia east of the advancing frontier, were for the great part slaughtered and expunged. Only those able to travel rapidly enough in the right directions, the 'Flight to the Hills', survived to provide later generations of sub-Roman Britons. Simplicity is the main attraction of an interpretation which collapses in the face of evidence from various lines of study.

Alternatively it can now be supposed that wherever communities of Britons existed in the 5th century, Christian groups among them upheld their religion; and that even before 400 Christianity had been more widely diffused across Britannia than has been allowed. On such an argument, within that great swathe of present England unaffected by Saxon settlement until 500 or 550, an ecclesiastical presence of wholly Romano-British origin should be considered.

No single explanation fully covers all the circumstances yet observed. For instance, in southwest Britain (Devon west of Exeter, Cornwall and the Isles of Scilly) there is virtually no evidence of popular Christianity before the 6th century. Here, given the proximity, through Brittany, to Christian Gaul, a measure of European influence is geographically likely and historically supportable. The case is quite different for southern Scotland (Chapter 5), where non-Saxon northern England south of Hadrian's Wall must have been the source.

Even within 5th-century Britannia, and earlier than whatever event was represented by the Adventus Saxonum, there are illustrations of interest. Far from dissolving itself after 410 or any other seminal year of crisis, the British Church was embroiled in a purely theological dispute, between orthodoxy and the heresies concerning free will of Pelagius – a philosopher, British in origin, who was prominent in Mediterranean circles. It became necessary for bishops elsewhere within the Gaulish prefecture to intervene. Victricius of Rouen paid a visit, though for unknown reasons, in the 390s. In 429 Germanus of Auxerre, the leading churchman in Gaul, and another bishop, Lupus of Troyes, were asked to help combat the Pelagian heresy. A late 5th-century account shows the two as preaching widely in southeast England, confounding heretics, on one occasion organizing a battle against a Saxon band (before his conversion and episcopate, Germanus – a remarkable person – had been a lawyer, and then a provincial military commander) and also visiting the shrine of St Alban. Here what must even then have been a standing church of note lay outside the Roman city (Verulamium), its origin being the martyr's grave in one of the external municipal cemeteries. As late as 448 Germanus paid a *second* visit, related by his biographer as being for similar ends and with similar and even more decisive results. Everything we know of the Christian hierarchy at this period tells us that any such event implies formal requests by church councils or synods, and therefore (somewhere in Britain) a functioning ecclesiastical system.

St Patrick

Paradoxically, much information may be gleaned not from internal British sources but from the career of St Patrick, national apostle of Ireland. It resides in his two surviving writings, both known in what seem to be very early and genuine guises – a 'Letter to the soldiers of Coroticus' and the later and longer *Confessio.*

Patrick or Patricius was a Briton. His father Calpurnius had been both a Christian deacon and a decurion, holding an obligatory civil office that implies he was a Roman citizen of standing and wealth. A grandfather, Potitus, had been a Christian priest, the grade above that of deacon. When Patrick was about sixteen he, together with some male and female servants, was captured by Scoti – Irish raiders who attacked his father's country estate. He spent the next six years as a slave, an unfree farm-hand or shepherd lad, somewhere in Ireland, and slender clues suggest this was in the northwest of Ireland. Then, guided by a dream, he decided to escape, walked a very long way, reached a harbour (presumably on the southern coast) and was able to sail away in a merchant craft with a pagan crew. There was a three-day voyage, after which the whole party travelled overland for about a month, through a countryside partly forested and at the time deserted by its inhabitants.

Subsequently Patrick returned to his home in Britain; we do not learn how, or when. He underwent formal training in a Christian setting, was ordained a deacon (and probably at the age of thirty, a priest, though this too is not stated). He was chosen to be a bishop and in that capacity he returned to Ireland, as he put it, to become a slave for Christ among the people who had earlier enslaved him. He never left Ireland again. Once, possibly more often, he had British visitors. Patrick's career was unusual in that its main component was missionary work carried out in various districts of a then-heathen land. A bishop's duties at this period were, strictly, confined to the pastoral oversight of an existing and geographically fixed flock, a rule exercised from an episcopal seat (usually urban, certainly with one or more churches).

Patrick's activities were therefore markedly un-Roman. Ireland had its dynastic royal strongholds, but no towns or fixed administrative geography. There could be nothing corresponding to the church diocese, bishop's seat, and family of lesser clerics with known duties, safely to be expected in 4th- and 5th-century Britannia. If Patrick caused churches to be built we can only guess at their insubstantial nature. Whatever he did, in his interpretation of his Christian duty, was subject to considerable misrepresentation in Britain, and his *Confessio*, written or dictated in his final years, has a large element of self-justification.

It can be inferred that his first language was (Late) British; that in captivity, and again later, he must have known Irish well; and that he also knew Latin. This he could read, and memorize in written form principally from one early version of the Latin Bible. When he spoke, composed or dictated Latin, he did so in a contemporary style and with rather more difficulty.

The literature about Patrick is enormous, and it begins with Latin and Irish lives composed later than his own lifetime. These do not rank as primary evidence for the man and his career, though it seems safe to accept early statements that his mother was called Concessa, and that his

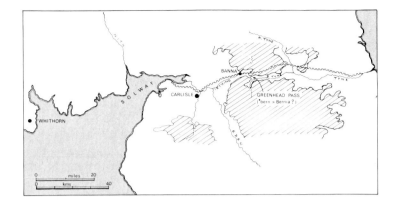

70–72 St Patrick
(*Above left*) Patrick, the
Briton, as Ireland's
national apostle and
Christian hero –
commemorative postage
stamp, 1961, the 1500th
anniversary of the
official date of Patrick's
death. (*Above right*) The
immediate geography of
Patrick's homeland,
early 5th century. If his
father's estate, read as
'Banna venta Berniae',
lay near the fort of
Birdoswald (BANNA) on
Hadrian's Wall, the
district 'Bernia' may
have been centred on
the Greenhead Pass –
British *bern* =
'mountain-pass'. (*Right*)
The wider world of St
Patrick, from his own
writings; included also
is the assumed route
(with times of travel) of
his escape from Ireland
to (?)Gaul at the age of
about twenty-two.

own additional Romano-British names had been Magonus and (in Irish) Sucat. His father's estate (*villula*) with its servants should have been linked to a house in whatever town or civitas centre supported the *ordo* or local council to which Calpurnius, as a decurion, was subject; and probably, too, the 4th-century church where the grandfather Potitus had ministered.

Though Patrick's importance as one of Celtic Britain's earliest churchmen stands out, his writings give no absolute dates and almost no geography. The two favoured datings would have him either born about 389, enslaved in 405, returning to Ireland as bishop in 432 and dying there in 461 – what might be called the official chronology; or else as having been born in the 5th century and captured in the 430s, returning to Ireland between 450 and 460 and dying soon after 490. Current scholarly opinion now favours the second and later sequence. The solitary place-name he quotes (*vicum bannaven taburniae* – with variations in early manuscripts) is of a place presumably near the western coast (in view of Irish raiders), within Britannia and so within the northern frontier, perhaps more or less opposite Ulster. The usual reconstruction of the place-name as *vicus Banna venta Berniae* points to a civilian settlement near Banna, the Roman fort at Birdoswald on Hadrian's Wall. *Venta* is an addition meaning something like 'local centre, market-place'. As at least one other Bannaventa is known, near Daventry in Northamptonshire, *Berniae*, 'Of-Bernia' will be a district-name added for precision. This identification greatly outweighs others put forward; and Luguvalium, Roman Carlisle, 15 miles west of Birdoswald, would be the appropriate civitas capital – of the 4th-century *civitas Carvetiorum* – with an ordo, town houses and we assume even a post-313 church.

It is the British, not the Irish, implications that open further. In such an area, well removed from the first English settlements, a landed Romano-British family exhibited three generations of Christian offices before and after 400. Patrick's schooling and later training, both in Latin, took place in the 5th century. As a youthful castaway in Ireland he would have been one of many British who played some early part in Ireland's Christianity. His sea voyage, offering a glimpse of maritime trade affecting Ireland, took him somewhere for a time – he calls it *paucos annos*, 'a few years' – that is more likely to have been northern Gaul than southern England, and it is argued that his command of colloquial Latin in old age shows the influence of a stay in a Gaulish Christian milieu.

There had been a previous missionary venture to Ireland (one that Patrick nowhere mentions) when in 431 Pope Celestine had sent Palladius, a prominent Gaulish deacon, to act as first bishop for an Irish community known to be Christian. Later depicted as short-lived, the venture is not to be connected with any part reached by Patrick, but with an east-coast region south of Dublin; and possibly with the Christian influences of earlier mercantile contact between Britannia and certain

Irish ports. But, where Rome and the papacy are concerned, we have no reason to see Patrick as answerable other than to the Church in Britain. In some 5th-century British region, one which ought to have contained Patrick's home, Christians could still be trained for the priesthood, consecrated (by other bishops) as bishops, sent to fulfil a supposed spiritual obligation to Christians and even to the unconverted in neighbouring Ireland, and if necessary requested to answer for their conduct to formal synods. And it is instructive to discover, analyzing Patrick's direct and implied statements, that he saw himself as having under God a total spiritual authority within his equivalent of a diocese, which in temporal terms lay in one or more Irish kingdoms whose rulers would have exercised equivalent secular command. When Coroticus – perhaps a mid-5th century Welsh king, or a slightly later king of the Strathclyde Britons, or simply an outlawed British prince operating in northern Ireland – allowed his war-band to enslave some Christian Irish converts, Patrick excommunicated the soldiers and the ruler alike.

Here then is the Church in Celtic Britain, functioning as late as the mid-5th century in a manner that seems not just to continue but to extend its 4th-century role. If we wish to anchor these inferences drawn from Patrick's career to sub-Roman geography, then Carlisle and the river valleys and Lake District southwards – Cumbria – was part of 6th-century Rheged; a British dialect (Cumbric) lasted here until late within the 1st millennium AD. Still in the north of England, the kingdom of Elmet was almost certainly Christian. Bede knew that there were or had been British Christians west of Northumbria and that Elmet contained *loca sacra*, 'holy places', if only as despised village churches of wood. Most mysterious is the sub-Roman status of York, where the combined military and civilian centre, Eboracum, capital of Britannia Inferior, is as we have seen a most likely centre for the sub-Roman British kingdom of Deira in its pre-Anglian period.

York was second only to the capital of the diocese, Londinium (Augusta), the official seat of the Roman *legatus Augusti pro praetore* or governor of Britain. Something of York's importance remained. When Pope Gregory despatched Augustine and his band, as a mission to the English race, to land at Thanet in Kent in 597, Augustine's instructions were to bring about an ecclesiastical structure (which persists today in the Church of England). There was to be a metropolitan primate at Canterbury, by then the capital of the Kentish kingdom, a second metropolitan at York, and a particular status for the see of London. Three decades later, the first Anglian Christian king of Northumbria built a church in what remained of the Roman headquarters complex at York (and archaeology shows us that a surprising amount did remain). Had York ever been totally deserted since the 400s? Was there still somewhere a titular bishop in direct line from the Eborius, bishop of Eboracum, recorded for 314? Were his followers entirely British or did they include

Anglian converts, won by the sub-Roman British Church before Augustine's successors reached the north? And finally, to round off these now permissible speculations, reverting to 460 or later, was any British synod (inferred from Patrick's later career) meeting within newly-emergent Rheged, or in Elmet, or under senior British bishops still able to convene a council at Eboracum?

Church organization in Celtic Britain

From the 5th to 7th centuries, accepting that the Church in Britain was mainly the continuation of its late Roman predecessor, we find two ecclesiastical structures, which became parallel and interconnected – the diocesan and the monastic. Quite apart from what may be inferred from Patrick's career, or read into the comments by Gildas in the following century, there were bishops; and this implies episcopal rule, even if the dioceses, the territories spiritually subject to each bishop, are nowhere apparent with any clarity.

73 Under York Minster: a massive column from the Roman legionary headquarters building. Excavations have shown that this did not collapse until the 9th century. Did sub-Roman British churchmen, as well as later Anglian kings, use any part of this vast building?

Augustine in 597, like his Pope, was aware that the mission to Kent and thence outward to the other English kingdoms would be set in a country that already possessed bishops of its own – *Brittaniae sacerdotes*. When Augustine wrote to Pope Gregory asking how he was expected to deal with these figures, he was told that though his status gave him no authority over the bishops in Gaul (who possessed their own metropolitan at Arles) he would, as the incoming archbishop for Britain, have papal authority over all the bishops of the British. A few years later, Augustine arranged a meeting with the bishops and learned men of what Bede calls *proximae Brettonum provinciae*, 'the nearest province of the Britons' – it goes too far to take this as meaning Wales only. No agreement was reached, and a second meeting, involving a delegation said to have come from Bancornaburg, Bangor-ys-Coed on the Dee in northeast Wales, also ended with the British declining to accept Augustine as the country's single spiritual overlord. Behind this, seemingly un-Christian, disagreement between two church parties who shared the same faith, forms of worship, Latin as a joint tongue and even Apostolic succession from St Peter and all subsequent bishops of Rome, one can glimpse a divide betwixt Celt and Saxon that the British were unable to cross. Over a century later, Bede was to record against the British (Christian) nation their awful failure to extend the Light of the Gospel to those, initially deprived of such salvation, with whom they had come to share the land of England. It is a strange quirk of history that, later than Augustine and his successors, conversion came to the English in the north from those *Irish* churchmen who were the descendants of Patrick's converts; in other words, indirectly from Christian Britain through the mediacy of once-pagan neighbours.

Other references to the Celtic British episcopacy are almost casual. Southern Scotland may have possessed something equivalent to a very loose network of dioceses, and chance affords us what seem to be the gravestones of a few bishops involved (Chapter 5). At this period the title *sacerdos*, 'priest', distinguished from the usual Latin word for a Christian priest (*presbyter*), should in most cases be read as 'bishop'. The oldest Lives of western British saints often describe their subjects as of episcopal rank. In Cornwall, Samson in the 6th century is shown acting as a visiting bishop and, at the same period, Paul Aurelian – wishing to travel onwards to the British in Armorica (Brittany) – refuses the Dumnonian king's plea to accept *pontificatum*, the bishop's office, in this particular realm. Dubricius, or Dyfrig, a slightly older figure (of early 6th-century south Wales), is invariably depicted as a bishop. For Celtic Britain generally the evidence is slight and patchy, however; even in Wales, where the emphasis upon the episcopacy was far stronger than in Ireland or other British regions, one can do no more than guess at the territorial extents and natures of their dioceses.

74 Moyne Graveyard, a small monastic enclosure near Shrule, Co. Mayo. Note the burial area and traces of internal divisions.

Early monasticism

In those European countries whose Christianity today descends, with or without a Reformation, from the western half of the late Roman empire, the basic ecclesiastical structure has also been inherited. Sees of dioceses are anchored to cities of great antiquity, archbishoprics hold fast to equally early metropolitan locations, bishop-lists (their earlier parts possibly genuine) go back to founder figures at least as old as St Patrick and the structure has tended to outlast most political groupings. For Britain, it can only be claimed that England retains (with its Canterbury, York and London) nearly all of the 7th-century system laid down by Pope Gregory and initiated by Augustine. British Christianity otherwise experienced a two-fold interruption from the far less secure 4th-century Roman British system – the national bouleversements of the 5th and 6th centuries, and the (pre-Viking) rise of monasticism.

75, 76 **Old Melrose**, an oxbow formation in the river Tweed, site of a 7th-century monastery; the inspiration here is typically 'Celtic' and *Mailros*, as Bede calls its, may have been founded from Lindisfarne. The simplified plan (*right*), from a 1961 field survey, shows the position of the vallum bank, and likely position of the monastic chapel.

77 Clonard, Co. Meath, site of St Finnian's monastery in the 6th century. Inner enclosure, upper right; there are also traces of a much larger outer enclosure, incorporating cultivated land within the monastery.

The differences between a late Roman urban Christian community with its own bishop, church(es) and cemetery, and a full monastery, lay in the degree of commitment to the Christian life; and stemming from this, the modes in which everyday living could be organized and degrees of withdrawal from the everyday world expressed and guaranteed.

A monastic community, at its ideal shape, was made up of a group of persons of the same gender sharing a life of Christian prayer and contemplation, indifferent to personal comfort, and adhering to a 'rule' or set of instructions handed down from a founding-figure. The community would possess its own internal head, an abbot or occasionally prior, who would be in clerical orders but not usually or necessarily a bishop. If a monastery produced its subsistence by low-level mixed farming it would require land, as well as a church, huts or living-cells and any communal buildings. Other activities could represent external contacts or physical growth – education, provision of visiting clerics for the district, establishment of outlying hermitages for solitary retreats and eventually the setting-up of daughter houses. These might call for grants by the mighty or pious of additional land. None the less the monastery

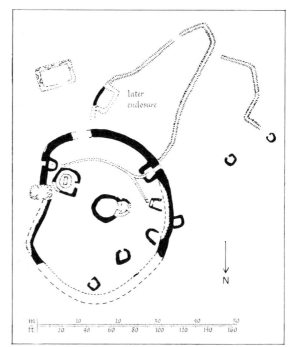

78, 79 **Monastic communities in isolated places** Sgor nam Ban-Naomha, or 'the Cliff of the Holy Women', on the Isle of Canna, Scotland. View of site (*below*) under bracken, from higher ground to the north, and plan (*right*).

itself could be considerably larger in area than a Christian Roman town establishment with its church, bishop's house, and plot. Spiritual separation might also be shown by the presence of one or more enclosures, containing the central monastic buildings and possibly bounding the amount of land required for immediate support.

This definition, where Celtic Britain and Ireland are concerned, is proper to the 6th century and later, and the field archaeology of such monasteries is briefly explored below. Here we must consider the origins. Not only did British monasticism ante-date Augustine's landing in 597; in Britain and Ireland it underwent its own development. Writing just before 731, not unsympathetically, Bede observed of the monastery at Iona which had been founded by Columcille or Columba in 563 that 'it always has an abbot for its ruler who is a priest, to whose authority the whole kingdom (of the Scottish settlers), including even bishops, has to be subject'. He adds that this is because Columba himself was a priest and a monk, but not a bishop; and he calls this *ordine inusitato* ('by an unusual arrangement').

From the earliest times in Mediterranean lands the solitary holy man, choosing to isolate himself in the desert, maintained under Christianity a tradition of the magical ascetic. The 2nd–3rd-century persecutions, occasional harshness of imposed Roman rule and awareness of a certain gulf between urban life at the top and Christian ideals, between them gave considerable impetus to the foundation of spiritual settlements in regions like Egypt and Palestine, preferably as far removed as possible from towns and travellers' highways. In this world of the Desert Fathers, where monasteries began to produce their own literature, to acquire fame, and to attract unwelcome fringe-settlements of followers and even traders, Christians from Gaul and Spain saw a central model of holy withdrawal from life in their own increasingly troubled provinces. If Nature failed to provide deserts, there were islands – little deserts in the sea – and remote valleys or dense forests.

Enthusiasts for the monastic life will have visited Britain before 400 – Victricius of Rouen was one such – and individual Christians no doubt vowed themselves to celibacy and ascetic living. Patrick himself speaks twice of 'sons and daughters of Irish rulers (as) monks (*monachi*) and virgins of Christ'. If these were his actual words, they point to 5th-century enthusiasts and converts from the well-to-do classes in his part of Ireland, but not necessarily to formal communities; he does not mention monasteries. As for Gildas a century later, there is admittedly a slightly larger volume of references, direct or indirect, to monastic life; but in reviling King Maglocunus (p. 51) for having espoused *monachorum decretae* ('the rules of the monks'), having vowed to become a monk, but then having returned to evil ways, Gildas appears only to imply a personal commitment. Its main implication was celibacy. Gildas brands the king's marriage, 'after your vow to become a monk had come to nothing', as illegal in Christian eyes. As Professor William Davies concluded some time ago, the monastic element in Gildas's Britain seems still small at the date when he was writing. Nor, looking northward, can it now be supposed that Ninian's 5th-century church at Whithorn (Chapter 5) was in any sense a proper monastery; monasticism here was a later development.

The general conclusion is that monasticism, if by that word we mean the rise of communities subject to fixed rules inhabiting monastic sites, characterized Celtic Britain only from the later 5th century. As an ecclesiastical structure it did not entirely replace whatever was retained of the older system involving territorial bishops. Professor Wendy Davies points this out particularly for Wales, where the degree of inheritance from late Roman Christianity was stronger than it ever was in Scotland.

How, then, was such monasticism introduced? Here we tread on most uncertain ground. Fourth-century Britons must have known that in parts of Gaul there were monastic foundations, ultimately inspired from the eastern deserts. The great, individualistic St Martin of Tours (who died in 397) created his own form of monastery in northwest Gaul, but other houses in the south possessed more conventional guises with communal rules, aristocratic yet saintly leaders and a high intellectual contact. It can be argued that one main strand in the appearance of monasteries in 6th-century Ireland was south Gaulish influence and that the extent of direct Irish-Gaulish contact after 400 has been underestimated. Similarly links (other than, and slightly later than, through Patrick) between Ireland and western Britain may have had something to do with the rise of the first Welsh monasteries. The much more tenuous connection, implicit in sea-borne trade and returning British or Irish pilgrims, with the eastern Mediterranean world directly – not mediated through Gaul, or Iberia – cannot be wholly dismissed. Archaeologically it is still the least unsatisfactory explanation for 6th-century details in Irish and British Christian art and architecture. Finally (as the late P. A. Wilson argued) monasticism in Ireland may have begun somewhat before 525 through the lead of St Finnian at Clonard, Finnian having been trained in the earlier monastery of St Cadoc in south Wales. Here, as in other western regions of Britain, small communities of resident clergy subject to vows and celibate life that – under Gaulish influence – had been known before 400 in the cities of Britannia were, with the collapse of Roman rule, 're-sited in places where they enjoyed the protection of native princes'. In the absence of towns the locations of these communities would tend to be in isolated places. In Celtic Britain as in Ireland, 'the incompatibility of the Christian life and the vanities of this world' and the diffusion of monastic ideas from late Roman Britain and neighbouring Europe jointly favoured a flowering, after 500, of monasteries by the dozens if not hundreds. Early monasticism in Britain, as in Ireland, may well have arisen from internal as well as external inspiration.

Church archaeology: an outline

Under Roman rule, both the physical face of Britannia and the assimilation of Christian organization to the existing order of government provided the Church with a setting we see elsewhere in the late empire. When town life failed and when native kingdoms with uncertain geographical foci replaced civitates and provinciae we can guess that provisions for Christian worship and burial must have taken entirely new shape.

For the early Christian, most of whose religious prospects centred upon the Resurrection and an eventual, possibly speedy, re-union of all kindred souls in Christ's Heaven, correct forms of burial were important. This meant interment in a duly consecrated cemetery, the skeleton being placed on a line east-west (head at the west end), and an absence of grave-goods or the token provisions deemed necessary in pagan afterlife. It is unfortunate, archaeologically, that during the Roman period there had been a shift from cremation to (pagan) inhumation – burial of the corpse – and that within Britannia there could very well be cemeteries with rows of burials, lacking grave-goods through sheer poverty and aligned east-west either through chance or the dictates of space, where neither the date nor the religious character is apparent. In fact a large class of these sub-Roman, rural, cemeteries is now known. Some may be entirely Christian, some only partly so, some arguably not at all.

The numerically smaller communities, inhabiting less populated tracts in the southwest, west and north, favoured in sub-Roman times small enclosed burial-grounds – frequently marked by walls or banks or ditches, which enclose little oval or near-circular plots – whose Christian character is not really in doubt. Occasionally they boast inscribed tombstones, or the first cross-marked memorial stones. In very many cases it seems that, since these cemeteries were the principal fixed Christian locales in what we could now call a parish or rural district, small churches were erected within them. Excavation can reveal that such churches, if built (say) in the late 7th century, are likely to be sited unwittingly and directly above burials of the 6th or even 5th century. The continuity of a great many such sites in Celtic Britain is remarkable and, allowing for the medieval and later rebuildings of the enclosure, present parish churches in southern Scotland, northwest England, Wales and the southwest still display what are essentially the local sub-Roman churchyards. As a Late British word, *landa*, had come to mean 'enclosure', its derivatives were used to name these burial-grounds and their contents, and eventually the settlements around them. Welsh place-names incorporating *Llan-*, Cornish ones *Lan-*, are explained thus, as we have seen. In Ireland a parallel development took place, employing a word borrowed from Latin *cella*. It is not clear precisely what this first meant (as Old Irish *cell*). Whether it referred to a marked-out

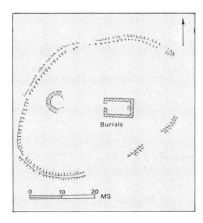

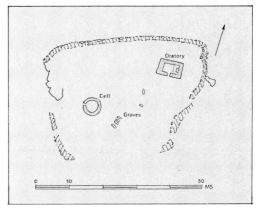

80–82 **Enclosed Christian cemeteries** (*Above left*) Ardwall Isle,
Kirkcudbrightshire, Scotland, developed around AD 700 with small stone church and
living-cell. (*Above right*) From the other end of western Britain: enclosed developed
cemetery (phase I, 6th–7th centuries) on St Helen's, Isles of Scilly. (*Below*)
Retention of the original circular enclosure into modern times: part of the inner
burial-ground at St Blane's, Isle of Bute, Scotland.

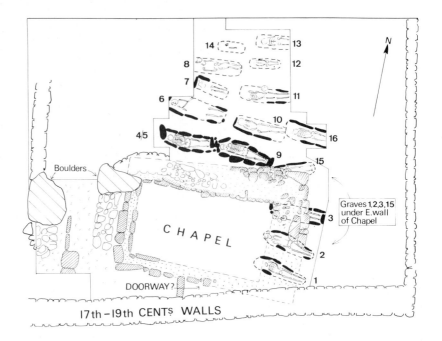

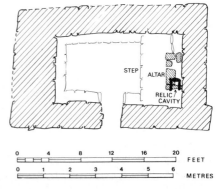

83–85 **The first churches** (*Above*)
Putative evidence of a smaller timber
forerunner, below a stone-walled chapel
on the same site: Tean, Isles of Scilly,
showing how the earlier graves partly
underlie the stone walls and avoid an
approximately rectangular area below
the chapel. (*Right* and *below*) Ground
plan and view of east end interior of the
small stone church at St Helen's
Oratory, Isles of Scilly, around AD 700.

'compartment' of land or a priest's hut (living-cell) attached to a first small church, or still retained one of its Classical Latin meanings as 'a single room or chamber in a temple', *cell* underlies hundreds of Irish place-names of the form Kildare and Killarney. Where Irish settlements in mainland Britain were Christian, this place-name prefix can be found instead of *Lan-*; hence such names as Kilmartin (Argyll), Kilmarnock (Ayrshire) and Cilrhedyn (Dyfed).

Insofar as we can classify 4th-century church buildings in Britain – separate structures, not just rooms or parts of houses used for worship – there is a real distinction between congregational churches within towns, perhaps with room for a hundred or so people, and rather smaller churches that occurred in cemeteries over or by the graves of notables such as early bishops and were hence *outside* Roman towns. For the 5th century, it is probable that congregational churches did exist at convenient rural centres, in Elmet or Cumbria for example, though the chances of identifying one through excavation are extremely thin. There was a tradition, part-native, part-Roman, of large-scale building in timber, seen in what we would now call barns, byres and stable-blocks on Romano-British estates. It is detectable in a few sub-Roman timber halls (appropriate to prominent persons; there was one at South Cadbury Castle); and by implication in church construction, because sizeable British wooden churches form the most likely model for similar churches in Ireland. Later than Patrick's time, these find frequent mention in early Irish sources, where there is no reason to see them regarded as anything out of the ordinary. Various Irish annals record, between 612 and 795, the burning-down of thirty-three of these, several described as of impressive size.

Very rarely, the excavation of the oldest-known small stone-walled churches – none of which can be dated before about 700 – has uncovered traces, in the shape of post-hole settings, of even smaller and obviously earlier wooden examples. Where such a clear sequence cannot for any reason be demonstrated, the detailed placing of burials (which, being earlier on the same site as a stone church, may well underlie its walls) can point to the likelihood of a timber forerunner, corresponding to an appropriate blank space among the burials.

The commemoration of individual Christian graves took several forms. Since early burials were not necessarily very deep, low mounds of displaced soil and stones would have served within the memory of a generation and it is entirely probable that boulders or up-ended slabs roughly marked one or both ends of a grave. However, by the latter part of the 5th century the inscribed tombstone reappears for selected persons – presumably landowners, prominent Christians and members of ruling families, though this can only be an intelligent guess.

Here, unlike similar tombstone sequences in the Rhineland and parts of Gaul, there is no real continuity with Roman Britain, where in any

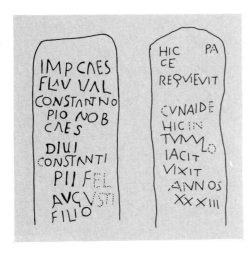

86–88 **Milestones and memorials**
(*Far left*) Roman milestone, early 4th
century, now at St Hilary church, west
Cornwall. (*Left*) A few miles to the
north, a 5th-century memorial stone of
Cunaide, from a site at St Erth. (*Above*)
A classic Early Christian memorial from
Liddel Water, Roxburgh, Scotland:
'Here lies Carantus, son of Cupitianus';
early 6th century.

event 4th-century (non-Christian) tombstones are actually uncommon.
The fashion, or idea, may well have come from outside; limited contact
with Christian Gaul is perhaps the best explanation. Lettering was at first
confined to Roman capitals which had been in near-universal use. A
knowledge of them does not necessarily imply full literacy; many artisans
who hammered out these inscriptions needed only to be able to copy
whatever pattern they had been given. Some minor part in all this was
played by one Roman survival, the milestone or road-marker, as the most
obvious rural display of Roman writing in horizontal lines. One or two
milestones were uprooted so that the reverse faces could be employed as
memorials, and the actual lettering on one late 5th-century tombstone in
west Cornwall seems to owe something to a surviving milestone a short
distance away.

The inscriptions are terse. The most widespread formula, as we saw in
the previous chapter, was no more than 'of A, of the son of B', using Latin
FILI for 'of the son (of)' and where the personal names were British,
giving them Latinized genitive endings. Common additions were short,
stock phrases like HIC IACIT ('here he (or she) lies'), IN PACE ('in peace')
and rather less often such nouns as MEMORIA ('the memorial of, the
Christian grave of'). An unusual, but classic, little series comes from the
remote island of Lundy in the Bristol Channel, where four such stones
still exist in a cemetery of sub-Roman origin, preserved by its isolation.
The oldest, possibly before 500, is really no more than a tiny grave-
marker with a single name added (OPTIMI – 'the grave of Optimus'), the
letters awkwardly split over three lines. Early 6th-century is the next,
with RESTEUTA (probably a British feminine name). Late in the century,
and now with the letters set sideways down a pillar, comes the grave of
Potitus (POTITI – the same name as Patrick's grandparent, see above); and
into the 7th century, a similar pillar, broken, with [CON]TIGERNI FILI
TIGERNI ('Grave of Contigernus, of the son of Tigernus').

89–92 **Chi-rhos and crosses** (*Right* and *far right*) Inscriptions headed by devolved chi-rho, encircled or plain: (?IUSTU)s and FLORENTIUS, Kirkmadrine, Scotland, around AD 500; and BROCAGNI, St Endellion, Cornwall, 6th century (with additional Ogham inscription). (*Below left*) Primary cross-incised slab, Iona, early 7th century. (*Below right*) Detail from primary slab with encircled cross, Ardwall Isle, perhaps after AD 700.

The Lundy stones introduce another element: the Christian ornament. There is a rough stone circle, like a large 'O', above the two-line Resteuta, quite possibly holding at the time of erection a painted device. One must not forget that Roman monumental slabs and inscriptions were commonly painted or picked out in bright colours and that, given the ease of making up mineral pigments, the Celtic British would have copied this. The name of Potitus, on his stone, is prefixed by a clumsy hot-cross-bun, a circle in a cross. The principal Christian device inherited from Britannia was the chi-rho, simplified from its 4th-century 'X and P' monogram to a plus-sign whose upper arm could be looped or hooked. This *is* found on certain inscribed stones, and the enclosing circle comes from one Roman version where, originally, the chi-rho was contained within a stylized *corona* or triumphal wreath.

While, fairly obviously, within the crude techniques of bashing lines on granite and similar stones with an iron chisel, a plus-sign with a small upper hook could very easily degenerate into a plus-sign alone, the Christian cross as a motif reached Britain and Ireland independently in sub-Roman times. It was not at first favoured by the Church, as being a direct symbol of Christ's passion and death through a Roman method of criminal execution. But by 400 or so, small initial crosses are found in many Mediterranean memorials, and by analogy they can head lines in Christian written texts. Somewhere and somehow, and one thinks of returning pilgrims on those merchant craft, this fashion reached Britain; importantly, one particular form (the double-outline cross with expanded arm ends) happens to be that used in basal stamps on class A fine red dishes.

Regions where inscribed tombstones are rare or absent – mostly in Ireland and the north of Britain – produced a kind of parallel, un-inscribed, tombstone series where linear or outline or encircled crosses take the part of an actual lettered statement. These 'primary cross-slabs' may go back to the early 6th century. Their appearance is significant because, simple as they may be, the *idea* of an upright stone marker bearing a prominent and unequivocal Christian device was one of several strands leading in much later centuries to entire regional schools of great freestanding decorated stone crosses – monuments whose ornament and sculpture drew otherwise on contemporary art styles in metalwork and manuscripts. And in addition to the cross, primary cross-slabs (with here and there, inscribed memorials) included in their own developed format other Christian symbols: a muddled memory of the Alpha and Omega, pairs of fishes or dolphins, even a totally unfamiliar pair of peacocks, as on a Reask (Co. Kerry) slab.

In Ireland, again apparently as an outcome of that 4th-century mercantile contact between Britannia and the Irish seaboard, a non-alphabetical form of stroke writing called Ogham, based on long and short dashes from or across a base line in groups of one to five, made its

The 'H' Surface

The 'B' Surface

HTDCQ

BLFSN MGNgZR AOUE I

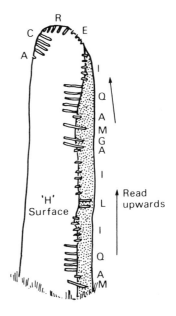

93 The Ogham alphabet: short and long strokes above, below, across and through the line – with an instance (*right*) from Co. Kerry, the tomb of MAQILIAG, son of ERCA.

appearance in late Roman times. Whoever invented it was familiar with the way certain Roman grammarians liked to classify letters, and the simplified technique is suitable for carving on rough stone. Rather similar memorial stones, the oldest being presumably pre-Christian but by the 5th century reflecting the gradual conversion of the Irish, are commoner in the south of Ireland. By 500 these are to be found wherever Irish communities had settled in Britain, mostly in northwest and southwest Wales, and in Dumnonia. Naturally the personal names are in a very early form of Irish, and the 'of A, of the son of B' formula used the Irish link-word MAQQI, 'of the son', instead of the Latin FILI. Of particular interest are those stones where both forms of writing appear and where, occasionally, the Roman capitals express Latin and Latinized British, and the Ogham strokes the slightly different Irish version. On the mid-6th-century tombstone of the Dyfed ruler, VOTEPORIGIS is accompanied by (in Ogham) VOTECORIGAS, showing how the -p- in the Late British element *wo-tepo-* was matched by a -*k*- sound in the related Primitive Irish *wo-teco*. Lastly, there are memorials entirely in Roman capitals where the actual name itself (like QUENATAUCI) is Irish and cannot, linguistically, be a British one.

Ogham words were either written on a drawn (or chiselled) baseline, or employed the up-and-down angle of a pillar or slab for this purpose.

Thus most Ogham writing is set vertically; this may be the main reason why, through imitation as well as slackness, many British epitaphs during the 6th and 7th centuries are similarly set out (compare the stone of Potitus, from Lundy). It has also been suggested that the essentially Celtic preference for giving the name of the deceased's father ('of the son of A') was popularized, in the British memorials with FILI, through the influence of Irish models with MAQQI. And crude as these several hundred sub-Roman and later inscriptions are, they provide us with more than just a glimpse of real individuals; they form a major source of information, despite the use of archaic forms, about the evolution of British into its daughter-tongues.

It is impossible to pursue the problem of why only certain people rated inscribed memorials. Even if 90 per cent of them have been lost through time, it is quite clear that memorials were confined to a minority. Allied to this is the question of what are sometimes called 'special' or 'specially marked' tombs. The Early Christian world laid far greater stress than does modern Christianity on the imminence of Christ's second coming and the Resurrection, and hence on the importance, physically, of those burials unquestionably destined for participation: burials of the first bishops of localities, martyrs under Roman persecutions, and outstandingly holy persons – *sancti*, saints – at whose tombs, and through whose intervention with God, miracles were agreed to occur. Celebrations of a sort we might now regard as curious were held, both at such graves and in small funerary chapels or memoriae built over and around the tombs, the upper surfaces of which could even be used as altar-tables.

This 'Cult of Martyrs' attained its peak in Mediterranean lands. A *martyr* (the original Greek word and its initial Latin borrowing meant 'witness') was not simply one put to death for professing the Faith, but a person steadfast under suffering and persecution, and before the 4th century most local Christian leaders and pioneers could, after death, be so venerated. The importance of the martyr's tomb in the whole development of Christian architecture is enormous. The magnificent cathedral church or 'abbey' at St Albans almost certainly originated as a small Roman-period structure over the grave of the local 3rd-century martyr Albanus, and the very hub of the Church – St Peter's, at Rome – has as its nucleus the 1st-century tomb of the Apostle Peter.

We do not know to what extent this practice had characterized Britannia by 400 (St Alban's apart). A century-and-a-half later Gildas implies that other such centres existed, even if the partition of Britain between Saxon and Briton meant that 'our citizens' were deprived of the opportunity to visit certain of them in English-settled areas. Gildas mentions two other martyrs, Aaron and Julius of *Urbs Legionem*, probably to be taken (as Bede supposed) to mean the legionary fortress in Monmouthshire, *Isca* (or *Castra Legionis?*), now Caerleon. In most of

Celtic Britain, however, the absence of both towns and the municipally maintained pagan or Christian cemeteries alongside them led, necessarily, to a different development.

Prominent sub-Roman Christians were commemorated in several ways. The elevation of tombstones has been explored; and exceptionally a man might be proclaimed as *sanctus et praecipuus*, 'holy and of outstanding excellence'. The popularity from the 7th century of the literary compositions we know as 'Lives' of various saints is another factor, since such a Life was linked closely to promoting visits to, and veneration at, the actual grave of the saint in question. Archaeologically we can find, in the 'specially marked' tombs, an early physical counterpart. Within certain enclosed burial grounds one or more graves may be distinguished, not only by an inscribed stone or a slab with a simple cross, but by some kind of surround, or a little construction designed to afford recognition at above-ground level. The surround may be a rectangular setting, a 'fence' of slabs and boulders, and in a few cases a circular one – the latter possibly a survival of pre-Christian custom, since there are Roman and Iron Age burials with circular surrounds (and indeed the connection between circular-plan ritual monuments and burials goes back, ultimately, to barrows and cist-cemeteries in the Bronze Age). The grave itself, at the time of burial a person-length trench in the ground lined or unlined with slabs, could be rendered more permanently visible with some form of stone superstructure. This may be (mainly in Ireland) two slabs meeting like a tiny stone ridge-tent, with triangular end-pieces; or perhaps an altar-like block of dry-stone masonry about a metre high, though it is less certain that such a structure necessarily always covers a grave.

The point is however that these specially marked graves of Celtic Britain (and Ireland) are outdoors. They did not, in the absence of any appropriate context or architectural tradition, give rise to sequences of churches of which they formed the primary core. In this respect they are, archaeologically, yet one more peculiarity of the British story. Nor is it very clear how they began, since it would be difficult to see the fashion as derived from anything we know of Roman Christianity in Britannia. Within the distinctively Christian sector of an enormous late Roman cemetery at Poundbury, Dorset, just outside the Roman town of Durnovaria (Dorchester), some graves were enclosed in little rectangular mausolea, masonry chambers with entrances, about the size of a garden shed. These are no later than the 4th century and, while they hint at the kind of embellishment that might have grown around St Albanus's grave, any further architectural development was cut short after the end of Roman rule in Britain.

The sub-Roman special graves, none probably older than 500 (or later), are conceivably inspired by Mediterranean, North African and Spanish models. The reasoning behind such a statement includes, once again, the chance that persons returning with occasional trading-ships from the East introduced the notion, as proper to a cult of the martyrial tomb witnessed at first hand elsewhere. There is a general similarity to *memoriae*, grave-surrounds or funerary chapels, as these had evolved in Mediterranean lands. In Britain a secondary treatment of the notable Christian dead arose, rather closer to Continental practice, but not at all widely before the 7th century. If, St Alban's being the main exception, Britain lacked examples of the sequence in which a church grew around a small early structure, enclosing some martyrial tomb in a 4th-century cemetery, this was mainly because, after the early 400s, the necessary setting of urban life and any continuing masonry building tradition could not provide the means to express what, on the Continent, took place in cities like Trier, Lyon and Geneva.

Accordingly, we have examples where the burial of a bishop or saint is a separate element; it takes place within, or in a slightly different way is removed to within, an already existing church. There are many instances in England after the conversion of the Anglo-Saxons, starting from Augustine's death at Canterbury and related by Bede in connection with a great many places, including Lindisfarne, Jarrow, Monkwearmouth, Lastingham, Beverley, Ely and Rochester. In Ireland a substantial timber-built church at Kildare was claimed, by the 7th century, to hold the tombs of St Brigid and a bishop. Presumably in the small churches of western and northern England, as of Wales, this could occur. The excavations of a few (post-700) small stone churches commonly reveal graves which were either older than the church, and could therefore lie below it, or were inserted at or soon after the time of building. Those which adjoin an altar are the more likely to represent such significant insertions but, almost invariably, one can do no more than guess at the occupant.

The removal of a saintly skeleton from its grave, and the transfer of the remains to what amounted to a new tomb visible and accessible above ground-level, was part of a further practice, the 'cult of relics'. The early Church may frequently have been ambivalent about this custom, but in many areas of Europe Christians themselves generally believed that a holy person's bones – and by a logical extension any part of a skeleton (skull, finger-bone), any object worn or handled by a saint and even components of furnishings or of situations closely associated with him – possessed a kind of spiritual power outlasting the subject's death. This power was most commonly manifested as having the property to cure disease or to heal injuries, but also to deflect fire and tempest, to ward off enemies and to force wrong doers to confess. In order to make the most potent of all such relics, the actual physical remnants, accessible to the devout, a burial originally concealed below ground had to be translated into some other form of tomb where – by raising the cover, or by inserting one's hand through a side-aperture – contact could occur. Where a skeleton had been dismembered, individual parts of it, and also any relics other than skeletal ones ('incorporeal relics'), were housed in large and small containers that might be venerated and opened up to allow the contents to be touched.

Shrines, as they are known, thus became Christian monuments, fixed or portable, in themselves. They afforded yet another whole field for the development of Christian ornamental art, particularly when after the 6th century the smaller portable shrines could be executed in bronze, silver, or silver and gilt, with semi-precious stones as added embellishments. The enshrinement of a complete skeleton, requiring as it did either a body-length container or at minimum an internal space long enough to accommodate the longest bones (femora, thigh-bones), was carried out in either wood or with stone slabs. Wood rarely survives archaeologically and the only known early instance, Anglian and not British, is the inner wooden chest with surface decoration made in 698 to hold the enshrined remains of St Cuthbert at Lindisfarne. Stone is permanent. The out-of-doors, tent-shaped grave covers of stone slabs ('slab shrines') mentioned earlier, found mainly in Ireland and associated with rectangular settings of stones may, if ultimately inspired from the East, be distant copies of the heavy ridged lids of late Classical Christian sarcophagi; huge one-piece stone coffins, with separate fitted covers that could if necessary be hauled up to permit access.

Stone shrines in Britain, composite constructions of great interest, are somewhat later in date (around 700 and afterwards). Their main characteristic is the use of side-slabs and end-slabs, which are roughly slotted into grooved stone corner-posts, the lid or cover being presumably a larger slab shaped to fit. The whole affair was held rigid through being footed in compact ground or being steadied in, say, the angle of a church wall interior and the fixed masonry block below an altar surface. This may look like a woodworker's 'tongue-and-groove' jointing technique transferred, clumsily, to stone slabs and pillars. In fact it copied rather similar methods for joints, current over centuries in Classical Mediterranean architecture and masonry and seen in the construction of *ambones* (pulpits), low solid screens and the surrounds of baptistery cisterns. This was practicable, using marbles and related materials that permitted close, regular shaping. Translation of the technique to the coarser rocks of Britain was less successful.

Inevitably, then, the appearance of such composite or 'corner-post' shrines, with their tendency to decorated surfaces and their presumed sitings indoors within churches, followed the contacts established between western Europe and the Mediterranean and the converted English kingdoms after Augustine's mission in 597 – mostly after the early 7th-century conversion of Northumbria. Examples (late 7th or early 8th century) from Pictish Scotland have to be explained as the outcome of Christian Northumbrian influences, not as of Celtic British origin. But, especially in northern England and in parts of Scotland, the suspicion remains that ways of providing accessibility to saintly graves and subsequently methods of enshrinement were known to the British through independent contact with Christian Europe. It is the conflation of the two streams that gives rise to (for instance) the remarkable ornamented stone double-shrines from 8th-century Shetland. As for the entire popular rationale underlying beliefs in the efficacy of relics, one can only point out that this is less a matter of direct Biblical doctrine than of a deeply rooted folklore, something no doubt inherited from pre-Christian times by Celt and Saxon alike in the setting of later prehistoric Europe. Possibly it is not just because we happen to lean so heavily on Bede's Northumbrian-based writing, but also because in Northumbria the British and the Angles seem to have undergone a degree of merger, that the most extreme instances are recorded from the 7th-century north. When the Christian ruler Oswald was killed fighting a pagan enemy in 642 his head and arms were barbarously cut off and fixed to stakes on the battlefield. Parts of Oswald's body were enshrined at different localities – the skull at Lindisfarne, the right arm (encased in a silver shrine) at Bamburgh – and the remaining bones taken to Bardney, Lincolnshire. All such portions and indeed all objects at any stage in contact with them shared the same miraculous power, as it might be like radioactivity or some permanently wet paint. The stake on which his head had been placed thereby became a relic in itself; later, an Irish monk was cured of plague by drinking water in which a chip off the stake had been soaked. At Bardney, the water used to wash Oswald's bones had been poured away in a corner; earth from the same spot was used to cure those possessed of devils. Some of the water, in transit, had been spilled on a stone pavement; and dust, swept up from this pavement when dry and collected in a little bag kept in a box, was used to cure an epileptic.

This shows us a climate of faith which may seem difficult to grasp today. It becomes slightly less difficult to accept if one thinks of the high prices realized at auction for one class of latter-day relics, the trivia associated with show-business personalities. There is no less a relic-cult of Elvis Presley than there was of St Columba, and the outlined heads of the Evangelists on St Cuthbert's oak reliquary-coffin have to be seen (in terms of comparative religion) alongside the mosaic portraits of John F. Kennedy and Padraig Pearse inside Galway's new Roman Catholic cathedral.

In conclusion, a little can be said about altars. Churches in the Roman period possessed altar-tables. The upper surface was regarded as consecrated, or else it seated a smaller, consecrated, slab (*mensa*) to act as a base for the holy vessels during the celebration of the Mass. In the few British instances the altar-table probably stood centrally in the east end, well away from the east inner wall. In those Celtic British churches about which we know anything, the smaller internal dimensions led to a

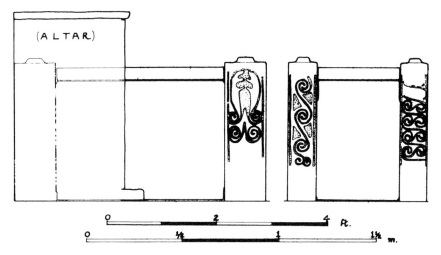

94 St Ninian's Isle, Shetland: the early 8th-century composite stone Shrine A (side and end view), in its original single form, as it stood against the south side of an altar in a contemporary chapel. The scheme of ornament involves Pictish 'S-dragons'.

different placing, with the altar – a masonry block about a metre high – built against the east wall's face. It is likely that, even in wooden churches of sub-Roman Britain, the altar's top at least was of stone; and Bede mentions just such a case at *Campodonum* (site of some Roman fort at Leeds). Here about 630 a wooden church was built by Paulinus, a successor-figure from Augustine's mission, for the rulers of Deira who had by then taken over the former Elmet. Whether this early Anglican church replaced a British one we cannot tell, but when it (and the royal dwellings) were burnt by heathens 'the altar escaped the burning, because it was of stone' and in Bede's day this slab was still preserved in an Anglian monastery *in silva Elmete* ('in the forest of Elmet').

The field archaeology of monasteries

Earlier it was hinted that the separate identity, the sense of 'apartness' from the world, of a monastic establishment could be given shape by some kind of enclosure. Precisely where this began first is a matter of debate, but the oldest monasteries in the eastern Mediterranean, where some extensive walled precinct of antiquity or former military work was not available, became surrounded by high mud-brick or stone walls. Privacy, the protection of fruit- and vegetable-plots from dusty winds, and defence against casual marauders were the requirements. Off the south French coast small islands, like Lerina (Lérins, near Cannes), were natural sea-girt enclaves.

In the British Isles, enclosures, walling-off or delineating or ramparting an area of at least a few acres, existed either as hillforts and cliff-castles, deserted since prehistory, or else as the left-over military works and coastal fortresses constructed by the Romans. We can only guess that as items of prestige or aspects of non-agricultural land they were at the disposal of native rulers, since early Lives of Irish saints, and from the 7th century those of English saints as well, relate how kings made these convenient enceintes available for monastic founders. Many examples are known. Coastal promontories, and inland ones – for instance, as at Old Melrose, an oxbow bend in the river Tweed – could serve. It is probable that (as indicated in saints' Lives, mostly known to us from medieval redactions but containing genuinely early material) smaller enclosures could be built over a few years either by a community or by hired gangs of itinerant diggers.

Our knowledge of what could lie within a monastic enclosure comes from partly excavated sites, or remote Irish houses where time has largely spared the original stone structures. At least one church, with a cemetery for the community, would be accompanied by a series of individual living-cells; in pre-Viking times, usually circular stone huts of older native type. Larger buildings imply communal purposes, like a guest-house, eating-chamber, infirmary, even a school.

There is a gradation down to what must still be seen as monasteries, even if they lack historical documentation, but only large enough to involve a tiny church and perhaps three or four cells. These, together with the ultimate in spiritual isolation – a single oratory and living-cell, adjoining and superficially enclosed in a wall or bank – are reflections of a theme common in saints' Lives and other literature: a further withdrawal from monasteries (which, in the 7th century, may occasionally have become more like private townships than copies of the Eastern originals) into communal or individual hermitages. In Britain, small islands offshore or occasionally in lakes formed the favoured venue. The parallel evolution of all kinds of monastic sites in Ireland and in Britain arose from a more or less common background of field archaeology. One difference – the presence in England and Wales of late Roman masonry shore-forts – can be illustrated, as when Maglocunus or Maelgwn of Gwynedd traditionally granted the short-fort near Holyhead, Anglesey, to St Cybi for a monastery. After the conversion of the English, similar forts in the southeast were granted to other saints by Saxon kings. It is worth mentioning that this re-use of Roman-period secular enclosures is also known from western Europe.

For the rest, up to 700 or so there is no real distinction in the treatment of burials, special graves or the modes of commemorating the dead as between monasteries and other Christian sites. Our knowledge of early Celtic British, and of Irish, monasticism is mostly literary and inferential, and very few large excavations have taken place. As a field of study, the origins and the early stages of these monasteries, together with their economy and significance in a post-Roman landscape, still offers a very considerable challenge.

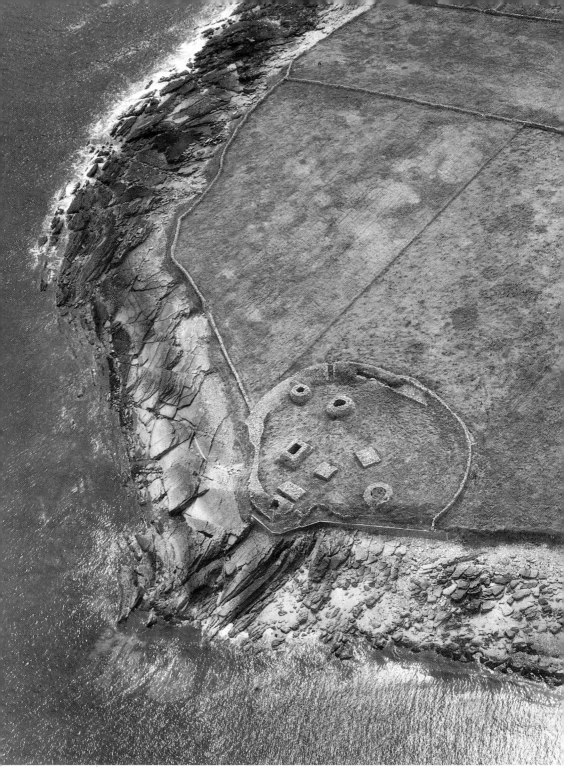

95 Holy isolation – the tiny monastic settlement with oratory and cells (restored) on
Illauntannig Island, off Co. Kerry, Ireland.

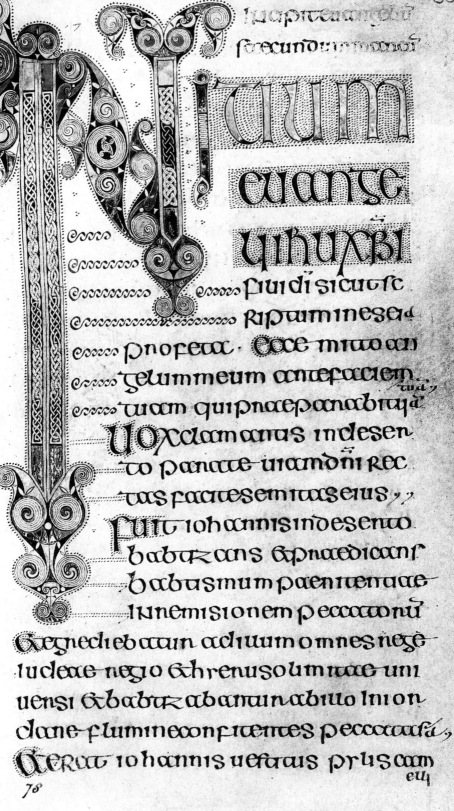

INITIUM

euangte

lii ihuxpi

fili di sicut sc
riptum in esai
propheta · ecce mitto an
gelum meum ante faciem
uiam qui praeparabit uia
Uox clamantis in desen
to parate uiam dni rec
tas facite semitas eius ⁊⁊
Fuit iohannis in deserto
babtizans & praedicans
babtismum paenitentiae
in remisionem peccatorum
Egrediebatur ad illum omnes rege
iudeae regio & hierusolimitae uni
uensi & babtizabantur ab illo in ion
dane flumine confitentes peccata sua ⁊
Erat iohannis uestitus pilis cam
eli

8·Art

ELTIC ART has long been big business. The Dublin-based Gaelic Revival at the end of the last century, and in Scotland a related though far less political movement housed in Glasgow, discovered (rediscovered?) a half-remembered world of art. Interlacings, triple or quadruple motifs, hints of strange animals and birds, wispy tailings-off on the perimeters, and a vague flavour of William Morris and the Kelmscott Press – all this was mingled with enthusiasm and greeted as appropriate to any fresh assertion of a Celtic past. The neo-Celtic style continues. It will do so as long as silversmiths have to meet a touristic demand for 'authentic' Scottish brooches, or folk-musicians want to design posters; now, there is even a Celtic-looking alphabet available in most ranges of press-down lettering.

Archaeologists, at the risk of being spoilsports, can only tell the truth as they see it. The material just described is not Celtic in the sense of having been exclusive to Celtic-speakers, or originating free from cultural contamination in wholly Celtic lands. There is, as prehistorians know, a Celtic art, but one proper only to the final centuries BC in central and western Europe. It represents a response by peoples of Late Bronze Age origins to two major stimuli. One was the chance offered with bright surfaces of bronzework to display symbolic and visually exciting designs, engraved and plastic; the other, the existence of a much more naturalistic and fully developed art – on every kind of medium – among the neighbouring Mediterranean civilizations.

Immediately before the Roman conquest of Britain a selective strain of Celtic art did reach both Britain and Ireland, with new immigrants and new trading contacts. At a popular rather than chieftainly level, something of this was maintained at a 'Romano-Celtic' standard of taste and execution during the Roman centuries. The supposedly Celtic art of modern tastes, of the Abbey Theatre and the Glasgow arcades, is also the outcome of stylistic fusion, but one belonging to a much later time. The Germanic settlers who, between the 5th and 8th centuries, created England within Britain had an art of their own. Transalpine and northern European in emphasis, it had also arisen with the ornamentation of traditional products in wood, metal and bone (and, presumably, in more

96 Opening page of St Mark's Gospel, from the 7th-century Book of Durrow.

transient media), and it too showed certain Classical influences at a remove. Within the framework of Christianity and by the middle of the 7th century, ecclesiastical and even royal contacts between Ireland, the Irish settlements in Scotland and Northumbria (perhaps, though more limited, between Anglo-Saxons and Britons in Britain) led to the emergence of new ideas and fresh expression of them. From the later 7th century, we can talk about 'Hiberno-Saxon' art. Such products as the Lindisfarne Gospels – in one light magnificent, in another superb but over-fussy and naive – and a host of 8th-, 9th- and 10th-century masterworks provide the basis upon which, uncritically, many modern conceptions of 'Celtic' art have been raised.

Presumably the Celts, as earlier defined, did have an art of their own during the 5th and 6th centuries; decreasingly so in the 7th as well. Judged by the severe standard of artistic appreciation, not all of it can rank for long with Iron Age Celtic art, nor with the main products of the Hiberno-Saxon world. In this present century much time and effort has been devoted to problems of Late Celtic art, as it has been called; its recognition, a clear definition and also its clear separation from any work of the pagan Anglo-Saxons. For, at one end of a scale, it becomes almost impossible to differentiate (unless with groups of finds in good contexts) between Celtic British or Irish or Pictish or Saxon workmanship. This is so with knives, the simpler combs, certain sorts of pin and many everyday products, all static in design and function, originating in a general Iron Age spread perhaps modified by Roman technology. Half-way up this scale, modest ornamentation appears. At the summit we can start to talk about artistry and craftsmanship. Consequently, for Celtic Britain, the progress of art is more readily traced in the work of the stone-carver and sculptor and eventually in that of the literate scribe, but the humbler items must be noticed first.

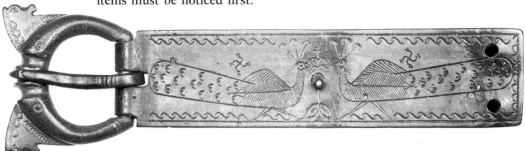

97 Late Roman bronze buckle, from Tripontium (Cave's Inn, Warwickshire), with peacocks and 'tree of life', probably a 4th-century Christian object.

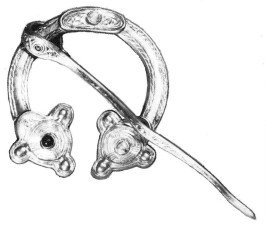

98, 99 **Brooches and pins**
(*Near right*) Developed
penannular brooch – silver,
8th century, from the St
Ninian's Isle hoard, Shetland
– showing how the ring-head
of the pin can travel around
the circuit of the brooch itself.
(*Far right*) The opposite of the
penannular – the 'stick' pin.
Silver hand-pin, 6th or 7th
century, from Scotland.

Metalwork

Most of this must be viewed as personal adornment. Circulating in 4th-century Britannia was a class of bronze buckles and belt fittings, often openwork (pierced or cut to internal shape including animal heads), engraved, or punched with dot-and-circle designs. The fashion had spread from Roman Gaul and the German provinces, as Germanic soldiers or mercenaries served in Britain. Some of these pieces may be 5th century. Buckles did not figure prominently in Celtic Britain, where the girdle was commoner than the leather belt. Britannia was famed for her woollen cloaks and outer garments, and most devices for fastening clothing are actually pins.

There are two basic groups. The penannular brooch or pin is pushed through adjoining folds of loose fabric and held firm when the head, an incomplete ring or 'penannulus', is moved around through the pin's pierced top to secure the object. In course of time, penannulars gained their enlarged and flattened ring-terminals; or the terminals became bent back, or assumed bird-head and animal-head form. The best of the later instances, in silver as well as bronze, are richly decorative with inlaid studs and much fine detailing.

The second group comprises all the 'stick' pins – elongated pins of metal (including, occasionally, iron) and bone. Heads may have small swivel-rings, or be embellished with a row of linear pegs like knuckles (hand-pins), or bear facets or knobs. There are numerous varieties. Quite different are so-called latchets; a dress-fastener like a flat metal toggle with a discoidal head. The whole range of ornament on such small items is restricted. Insofar as one can put together a vocabulary of motifs, it was shown some time ago (by Elizabeth Fowler) that in essence these carry forward the tastes of late Roman work.

There is a dimension of colour, often overlooked. Bronze if new and clean is an attractive red-gold (pure gold is still sometimes mistaken for brass). Surprising amounts of silver seem to have been available in post-Roman Britain, and the Roman craft of enamelling, feeding the (usually red) vitreous paste into inlays on polished surfaces, not only continued but spread with trade to 5th-century Ireland. Those major and frequently illustrated highlights of later times – the Hunterston and Tara brooches, the Moylough belt shrine, the Ardagh and Derrynaflan chalices – are the outcome of combining skill, long craft traditions, inventive flair, the right materials and patronage. The centuries which led up to such post-700 masterpieces can, in terms of art, only be seen as the light before the dawn.

100 Open-work hanging bowl escutcheon from Faversham, Kent; the central cross, flanked by dolphins, strongly indicates a Christian element in either manufacture or use of the bowl.

Within the 5th to 7th centuries, however, we are left with one achievement, enigmatic but not to be dismissed lightly: the hanging-bowls, and the riddle of who made them, and where. The name for them is ours. The chief function of these objects, circular bowls of thin beaten bronze sheet (rarely silver) with three or four loops for suspension fixed to the rims, is unknown. If they held liquid, oil would suggest floating-wick lamps; water, a royal handbasin or some ritual church use. A form of chalice, with wine, has been less plausibly suggested. The rim-loop sheet metal bowl is a late Roman device. Our hanging-bowls are dated by rim form, and by the shape, details and ornament of escutcheons (strengthening-plates joining loops to bowls) and any base-discs. The date range of the late 4th or early 5th to 7th centuries, indicated by the Celtic ornament and enamelled or openwork treatment, is supported by context; most of the known bowls or fragments come from Anglo-Saxon graves. Prime among such finds is the splendid Sutton Hoo bowl, unique in having its freestanding, three-dimensional fish attached to the inside base. The precise dates of bowls and escutcheons is of less moment than clientship and purpose. The sample we have may be unrepresentative simply because preserved through the accident of burial. There is little

Colour plates   VI A silver chalice, 19 cm high, part of the hoard found in 1980 within the precincts of the monastery of Derrynaflan, Co. Tipperary, and probably dating to about 800.
VII The Lion of St Mark, an Evangelist's symbol, from the so-called Echternach Gospels, discovered in a monastery of that name founded in 698 by St Willibrord, an English missionary from Northumbria.
VIII An ornamental carpet page from the Book of Durrow, Irish or Irish-Northumbrian, late 7th century.
IX The medieval abbey of Iona, much restored in modern times, stands on the site of St Columba's early monastic settlement.

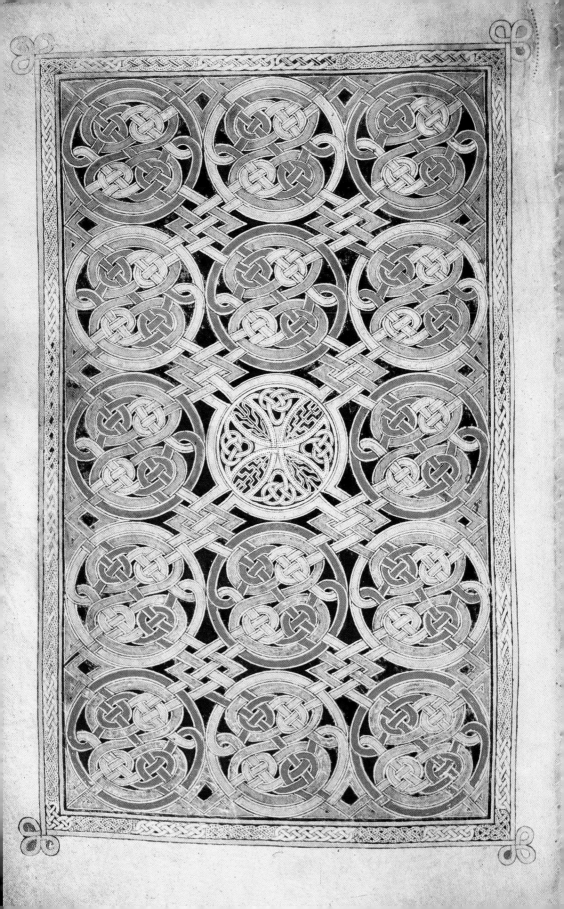

doubt that Celts produced them, but where? They cannot invariably be (as once supposed) of Irish origin; post-Roman British excavated sites yield more and more evidence (fine-clay moulds, crucibles) of metalworking on site, and we must allow that hanging-bowls were also produced in the north and west. We get no closer to any agreed solution through such new finds as the bowl from St Paul in the Bail, Lincoln. For unclear reasons the bowls, surely made for leading Britons (and British churches?), survive for the greater part after transfer to English hands. Were such bowls really as uncommon as the limited numbers imply?

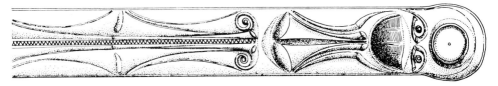

101 Caledonian metalwork, 2nd–3rd centuries AD. Detail of the heavy spiral bronze armlet from Culbin Sands, Morayshire, Scotland, drawn extended by Morna MacGregor. Behind the terminal snake-heads (with tiny blue-glass eyes), magical pointed horns reach back into the spiral.

Pictish art

The distinctive art associated with the Picts has roots older than the strictly historical emergence of that people (3rd century AD). During the Roman period and mainly in northeast Scotland we find certain objects lumped together as 'Caledonian metalwork'. Noteworthy are a half-dozen massive spiral bracelets, of three complete coils and with identical terminals, taking the shape of stylized snakes' heads, the mouths portrayed as flattened discs that would have held enamel inlay. With these are some twenty armlets of flattened heavy bronze, incomplete circles, assigned to the 2nd–3rd centuries AD and exhibiting very similar repoussé treatment along the length of each object. The material (and there are minor items as well), perhaps a local response to the stimuli of immigrant bronzesmiths, does not demonstrably stretch over the whole Roman period among those northern natives who were later to become Picts, but the snake-heads in particular, magical serpents possessing the horns of rams or goats, tell us that a plastic art had started to mirror pagan ideas.

Far in time behind these are the simpler arts of very much earlier inhabitants. There are nearly 400 carved stone balls, efficiently worked objects with flattened knobs, spirals and concentric circles, surely magical in purpose. Most come from what was to be the Pictish area. Though they originate in a local late Neolithic, we have no idea how late in prehistory others were produced or up to what stage they were still current as talismanic items. This concept of ornamental circularity is also seen, on a much wider and essentially public scale, in 'cup-and-ring art', the incising or grooving or pecking of circles, hollows, dots and lines on the surfaces of boulders or upon great slabs of exposed natural bedrock. A similar art is associated with post–Neolithic burials in cists – 'single-grave art' – and occasionally this includes depictions of axes of Bronze Age style, or human hands or feet. The distribution is wide but there is a concentration in Scotland and the northern parts of England and Ireland. The important thing is that all this rock art, then as now, was visible and could be copied. Whatever different significances might be read into the designs by early peoples, the absolute age of the workmanship would not have been a material consideration.

The various arts of the Picts of history must, other things being equal, be attributed to them because the vast majority of all examples occur within and are generally confined to the area known, on other and independent grounds, to have been the home of the Picts between the 3rd and 9th centuries. There is some metalwork, showing a development (in terms of size, complexity and degree of enrichment) from various pins and brooches of the Roman-influenced native Northern Iron Age. Late Roman silver appears to have been re-cycled to produce the remarkable Pictish chains, heavy neck ornaments presumably worn by men. Though none is securely dated in any good context, their limited distribution hints at Pictish ownership (and loss), possibly as late as the 7th century. The chains were fastened with large terminal-rings; two such (from Whitecleuch, Lanarks; Parkhill, Aberdeen) show incised and originally red-enamel-filled ornament. This ornament displays what are known as Pictish *symbols*, and we can use the fact as a starting-point.

The principal display of all such symbols occurs on stone, and the Pictish symbol stones are at one and the same time the greatest repository of true Pictish art, and still the outstanding problem in British protohistoric archaeology – more so than the origin of hanging-bowls. Conventionally we now group the stones into two classes, I and II. Class I stones are unshaped slabs or boulders or natural pillars, bearing on one or more flat faces the symbols incised in outline. Single symbols do occur (unless we regard them as broken fragments), but groups of two or three are predominant with, very occasionally, four. Class II stones are, in sculptural terms, more advanced. The slabs have been to some extent shaped or dressed, symbols may be executed in a low relief, though still having incised detail, and there is a wider range of ornament. Both sides of a slab can be used and there can be portrayals of human figures, groups of animals and fantastic beasts, as well as zones or bands of pure decoration. The most significant innovation is the appearance, dominating one face, of an evolved form of the Christian cross. The inference is therefore that class II stones are not only typologically an advance on, and thus *relatively* later than, those of class I; they are *absolutely* later (if historical dates can be adduced), in that they should

102 Pictish heavy silver chain with terminal rings decorated with Pictish symbols, recessed to take enamel; also, two silver plaques and a silver penannular brooch – from various Scottish sites.

have been set up in various parts of Pictland only after a conversion to Christianity.

Several hundred class I stones are known. Today, with the increasing erosion of remote tracts of Scotland by agriculture and forestry, new instances occur at an almost predictable rate of two every three years. On the assumption that distributional densities can point to origin-centres, it is held that the practice of incising and erecting the stones began in the northern Pictish area, around the Moray Firth and within the northeast coastal plain. There are some from further south, a handful from the Northern Isles, and three south of the Forth that point to isolated settlers or contemporary raids.

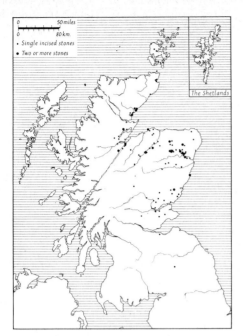

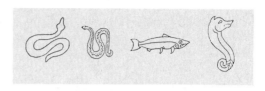

103–107 **Pictish symbol stones** (*Above*)
Distribution of stone slabs with class I
symbols, implying an origin in northern
Pictland. (*Above right*) The standard, and
perhaps earliest, Pictish animal forms – top
row: two snakes (decorated one used with Z-
rod), fish, S-dragon, cat or bear(?), wolf,
reindeer; second row: red deer (antlers
missing), hind(?), otter or seal(?); third row:
wild boar, bull, and white-tailed or sea eagle.
(*Near right*) Class I stone, Dunnichen,
Angus: flower over double disc and Z-rod,
with smaller comb and mirror visible below.
(*Centre*) Class I stone, Easterton of Roseisle:
goose above fish. (*Far right*) Newton,
Aberdeen: the double disc symbol, without
Z-rod, over the snake and Z-rod symbol.

The fifty-odd symbols are stylized, quite complex, outline shapes,
some with repetitive (and some with variegated) inner detail. The *animal*
symbols, it has long been recognized, portray a native fauna whose
existence at this period can be otherwise demonstrated: a salmon, a snake,
a goose, an eagle (the white-tailed or sea eagle), a wolf, a wild boar and a
red deer's head. There is a reindeer – these persisted in Scotland until the
early Middle Ages – a small horse and a short-horned bull, and there may
also be a hunting-dog and either a brown bear or wild cat. Two other
'animals' are unreal, the odd creature called 'the Pictish elephant', and
another ('Pictish S-dragon') with a dog-like head, fishy curved body and
spiral tail. They may embrace a contemporary notion of something not
totally visible on land, like a dolphin.

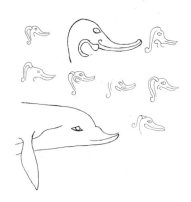

108, 109 **The 'Pictish Elephant'** (*Left*) On a stone from Strathmartine, Angus. (*Right*) Is the 'elephant' based on some notion of a dolphin? A series of 'elephant' heads, showing the curious beak, and (below left) outline of a dolphin's head from a Minoan fresco at Knossos, Crete.

Object symbols are numerous. One can divide them between many that depict actual and recognizable things – mirror, comb, hammer, sword, ring-handled cauldron with bar across and through the handles, etc. – and others that are abstract or, if very simple, just geometric shapes. The main abstract object symbols are known as the crescent, double disc, and notched rectangle. The crescent is mostly shown with a 'V-rod', a design rather like a broken arrow in V-form, superimposed on it; and the other two with a similar 'Z-rod', more like a broken spear, snapped but not divided into three lengths. Since all three symbols are also found without V-rod or Z-rod, the addition (or absence) of the extra designs must be deliberate, and similarly the snake symbol is found with a Z-rod added.

The symbolic art of the Picts, as seen on the class I stones, is unlike anything else in Britain. There is a broad, though fortuitous, resemblance to the *Bildsteine* or pictorial stones of southern Sweden, but these are distant and cover a different time span. The whole subject is full of riddles. If we look at Pictland north of the Mounth, the range of hills west from Aberdeen, this territory was in contact with Irish-derived Christianity stemming from Iona (and lesser centres). But a degree of popular Christianization sufficient to lead to class II stones – the shaped slabs with crosses as well as symbols – being erected in any numbers seems improbable before the late 7th century. The class I stones, as predecessors, might then belong to a period around 650 – period, not date, because the whole range suggests internal development through time – or possibly earlier; but how much earlier? One view holds that *all* Pictish symbol stones belong to the decades shortly before 700, and that the entire repertoire was inspired by contact with Christian Northumbria. And it is true that on class II stones one sees a resemblance at many points between Northumbrian art styles and the Pictish treatment of class II interlaced crosses, borders and decoratively enriched symbols.

110 Pictish class II Christian slab from Glamis, Angus; note the two symbols, lower right.

These may not be the right questions to ask, and it may help to look for something closer to first principles: where and how did the symbols, taken only as symbols, originate, and for what purpose or purposes were the class I stones ever set up? What can we learn from other, if admittedly unrelated, sets of stones carved with symbolic ornament in Europe in the centuries AD? Today, there is much support for the hypothesis that class I stones commemorate the Pictish dead, either as grave-side memorials or as monuments divorced from actual interments. This view allows us to by-pass any dating with reference to Christianity, because the symbols have no apparent Christian significance. Indeed, their inclusion on slabs with crosses might suggest that, whatever they meant, their meaning was not repugnant to the Faith. It does however extend the possibilities of dating by analogy. Picts raiding southwards in the late Roman centuries would have seen both pictorial and inscribed stonework along Hadrian's Wall, and could (still as pagans) have become aware that Christians were erecting both lettered and cross-incised stones in the Borders from the early 6th century, among the Dalriadic Scots by the early 7th. On balance it might be supposed that class I stones originated (by imitation) rather before 680, but hardly before 600. Note, though, that the vocabulary of *symbols* – which appear, already evolved and stylized, on the stones – may very well belong to an older period.

This is a powerful argument. The stereotyped shapes, confident execution and wide currency over so large a region all imply (with near certainty) that the symbolic repertoire was already common property. It could have been in existence for a long time. In support of this idea, it has been contended that some of the animal representations recall Iron Age traditions that must have reached Pictland with Celtic-speaking newcomers from the north of England, as well as owing something to the Roman use of mythological beasts on military and official slabs. Some of

111 Roman distance-slabs, with animals, on the Antonine Wall: Duntocher (*left*), and Old Kilpatrick (*right*).

112 A rare instance of surviving evidence for tattooing, in the manner suggested for the Picts: the permanently frozen corpse of the Scythian chieftain, barrow 2 at Pazyryk in the Altai Mountains, Siberia, 5th century BC.

the identifiable 'objects' are not necessarily the versions of tools and weapons in use by the historic Picts; on the contrary, they seem closer to their counterparts in the Roman period. Lastly, among the geometric symbols one finds distinct echoes of the fully prehistoric (but probably still visible, then, as now) cup-and-ring and single-grave art. These links, this backward-looking aspect, justify including a mention of Pictish art in a broadly Celtic study, even if one accepts that the Picts themselves were not exclusively Celtic.

Any postulated transmission of the core, if not totality, of the Pictish symbols from Roman times down to AD 600 would almost certainly have taken place in ways archaeology can very rarely detect. Symbols do appear (undated) on bronze, silver and stones, but generally in mature form. We could instead think of wooden surfaces, tooled leather and even textiles. A suggestion is that Picts painted or tattooed their faces, bodies and exposed limbs (which would as we saw in Chapter 5 explain the Roman name of *Picti*, 'the painted ones') and that by so doing they were maintaining in the far north a custom of great antiquity and former wide occurrence. There are Classical allusions to tattooed Caledonians and Picts, some admittedly derived from verse or prose statements with little or no independent weight. But in broader terms there are ample hints that tattooing was known, as early as the 2nd millennium BC in Europe and subsequently in the Mediterranean and Hither Asia. In Scotland tattooing may have been a pre-Celtic, pre-Iron Age inheritance; yet there appear to be tattooed cheeks on Gaulish coins, and we know of Caesar's remarks about the painted bodies of British tribes, while one post-Roman Irish source refers to tattooed shins.

An essential clue may lie here. If Pictish symbols did develop from tattoo devices with fixed meanings – taking on, in Pictland, nationally current significance from late Roman times – then by far the most likely meanings would be those concerning the status or rank, the group affiliation and the occupation of anyone bearing such marks. Later, and in the absence of any system of denoting qualities or personal details through writing, might not the marks be repeated on the equivalent of pictorial tombstones?

Agreement among scholars is unlikely and other theories exist, for example that the symbols fall into definite sets and were used – rather suddenly and for a restricted period – to announce marriage alliances or the giving of bride-prices, within a complex system of a sort familiar to social anthropology in other continents. It is at least common belief now that the class I symbols were disposed, or set out, according to guidelines which may not be explicable but seem to be in large part detectable. Most animal-symbol heads point to the right and, given the requirement of fitting two or three symbols on what may be an inconvenient rock surface, there is a tendency to see them as placed in vertical order. Now this does recall, at a basic level, the disposition of Roman and of Roman-derived memorials. Roman inscriptions have to be read, as we ourselves today have to read, from left to right and from a top line downwards. The decipherment of the whole system, the revelation in full detail of what any group of class I symbols may have meant to those who gazed at it, will always be beyond us and the very system hardly lends itself to more than a general statement. None the less one can suspect that the animals may hold a link with the subdivisions of the Pictish people, analogous with older tribal groupings having names of the type *Epidii* ('Horse-folk'), and that a hammer, anvil and tongs will – as on medieval Scottish tomb-slabs – be inherently more likely to imply a smith than a princess.

Pictish symbolic art, large-scale on stone, is not unique within Europe. Comparable (that is, artistically comparable) but wholly unrelated lithic styles have been studied elsewhere; for the Iberians in Spain, the Scandinavian *Bildsteine*, and the heretical Bogomil tombstones of medieval Yugoslavia. Pictish art is however unique in Britain and no other Celtic-speaking people developed so full a non-literate system at so late a stage. Taken with all the implications of survival, this underlines the mixed character of the historical Picts – outwardly, and in most respects, the stubborn Celts of the extreme north but with a component descended from far older aboriginals.

In his account of Agricola's defeat of the Caledonians at Mons Graupius, Tacitus puts words into the mouth of Calgacus, the native general. He is made to declare that 'Our very remoteness, and the general knowledge of our hidden obscurity, have preserved us until now – we, the furthest people of these lands, the Last Free Folk.' Poor Calgacus; his fictional oration was designed as a counterpoint to Agricola's ringing address to the legions ('Comrades . . . these remnant Britons are simply those who ran the fastest! That's why they are still alive!'), but there may have been more in Tacitus's phrasing than he intended. Pictish art arose within Pictish isolation, and there is little indication that it will shed its hidden obscurity.

Christian art on stone – the beginnings

Most people are familiar, if only from Ireland's tourist promotion of the spectacular Irish past, with the notion of High Crosses: tall, shaped, richly sculptured. There is a general idea that these must be 'Celtic' and the whole series of High Crosses has inspired countless war memorials and (notably in Scotland) outsized gravestones. The truth, however, is that their distinctive figured-scene art can be labelled Celtic only in the most loose sense of the word, and almost all the better-known examples are later than the Viking period.

The cross-marked stone or slab and its successor, the shaped freestanding cross, occur in much of Highland Britain and Ireland. Only the origins and early stages of these monuments fall inside the period covered by this book, and it is not always grasped that the origins are still problematical or that the artistic development was a gradual one.

Though naturally we associate the Cross, the Christian symbol *par excellence*, with the whole artistic world of the Church and the commemoration of the dead, it was by no means the earliest Christian motif. To the first Christians, it signified the Crucifixion; alone, it was a Roman instrument of execution. As we saw earlier, it does not appear in art in Britain until the 5th century and was uncommon until, probably, the mid-6th. The second (post-AD 400) version of the chi-rho device, with the older X P monogram simplified to a plus-sign (+) whose upper arm bore as a loop or hook the rounded element of the P, could be simplified to plain linear-cross form. It is quite probable that visitors from abroad, or British and Irish pilgrims returning from Europe and the Mediterranean, made known the existence of Gaulish or North African inscribed stones (mostly epitaphs) where small initial crosses were beginning to surmount or to precede the inscriptions.

By the 6th century, as we have noticed already, the tiny incised crosses occur on natural stones (with no inscriptions), and these *primary grave-markers* or primary cross-incised slabs are found in cemeteries. They will have been set upright or laid flat by graves. In Ireland, a subsequent series of recumbent stone slabs – their length and size extended as time passed – must have grown out of these beginnings, but in Britain development was concentrated rather on the vertical slab or pillar, the type of monument favoured of course on both sides of the Irish Sea for inscribed memorials, whether in Latin letters or Irish Oghams.

Linear crosses gave way to any number of elaborations, all within the capacity of a man with a chisel facing a flat surface. Lines were doubled to

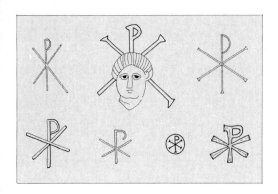

113, 114 **The evolution of the chi-rho**
(*Left*) Fourth-century AD forms from Roman Britain, in a variety of media. This first or 'Constantinian' form is common throughout most of the Roman Empire. (*Right*) The native development, 5th to 7th centuries – mostly the later 'hooked upright' form, plain or encircled, with or without flanking alpha and omega – in Insular art. Nos. 1, 10–12, 14 from Cornwall; 2–4 from Scotland (Kirkmadrine); 5 from Ireland (Co. Antrim); 6 and 9 from Wales; 7 and 13 from Devon; and 8 from a brooch.

form outlines open- or close-ended, the terminals (arm-ends) were expanded and given hooked or curled finials, and crosses were sometimes contained in circles. The last idea was probably copied from older depictions of encircled chi-rho, as on the Kirkmadrine slabs.

The main concentration of primary cross-incised slabs is decidedly northern – the northern two-thirds of Ireland, north Wales, the Isle of Man and (spreading from Irish settlement in Argyll and Galloway) the west and later north of Scotland. As such, it appears to complement the main concentration of all types of inscribed stones, to the extent that the *uninscribed* slab could be called the northern counterpart of the *lettered* (Latin or Ogham) stone with its much more southerly emphasis. The division preserves, in a very general light, the extent of any knowledge of writing as a medium of communication in the 4th century. There are, for instance, apparently no cases of the primary cross-slabs in southwest Britain.

Artistic elaboration through the later 6th and earlier 7th centuries was in many ways meagre. The stem or shaft of the cross can be elongated, the terminals floriated and the ring-head where present doubled, and there can be more than one cross per face. However, we find the occasional fresh motif, suggesting further external inspiration – chubby dolphins on a slab from Co. Mayo, facing peacocks on a stone from Reask, Co. Kerry – and coming presumably from the Christian iconography of the world outside.

Was this preliminary ornamentation the result of seeing decorated Christian objects that reached parts of Ireland and southwest Britain and were diffused northwards in the context of Irish settlements and their ecclesiastical activities? We cannot legitimately point to pictorial textiles – widespread at this era in Coptic Egypt and Mediterranean lands – or small religious paintings on wood, since none has survived. Another potential medium would be books: Christian manuscripts. From Patrick's day in 5th-century Ireland clerics there and in Atlantic Britain would have required texts with part or all of the Bible, along with service-books, the Psalms, commentaries and patristic writings. It is most

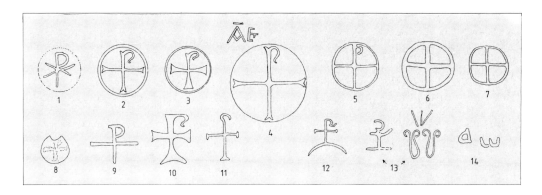

unlikely that, by 600, any such works inherited from 4th-century Roman Britain could have survived in enough numbers or sufficiently legible state to meet all subsequent needs through successive copying. From somewhere else – and we have to think of Gaul and Spain – fresh examples came to Ireland and parts of Celtic Britain. It is contended that Isidore of Seville's *Etymologiae*, a sort of fantastic encyclopaedia, was known in Ireland not long after its compilation in the early 7th century.

The texts of these Christian works, somewhat in parallel with the funerary epitaph tradition, began to exhibit ornamented capital and initial letters. As the flourishes grew, the borders and divisions were added and decorated and the ultimate step of insertion, as a wholly pictorial sheet or page, of what had been a separate religious miniature painting was taken. The great Western tradition of the fully decorative manuscript thus arose. And here is another potential source for further 7th-century embellishment of Christian art on stone. Peering ahead, momentarily, into the 8th century, it can be safely guessed that the addition of rectangular borders to Irish recumbent cross-slabs imitates the framed manuscript page. In the same period there are Pictish, Christian, class II stones where the fully occupied rectilinear scenic face is simply the stone equivalent of a decorated folio.

The initially slow development of Celtic British and Irish stone art reached a crucial point where the basic Cross motif 'escaped', as it were, from a flat and sterile depiction on a two-dimensional surface, to become shaped and freestanding. Apart from the confident statement that this occurred before the disruption of the first Viking attacks, and that occurrences should be sought in different regions at slightly different periods, we cannot say a great deal. The position is complicated by the fact that a parallel stone-monument tradition (after the 630s) among the converted Angles of Christian Northumbria experienced a similar leap forwards, probably within a generation one or other side of 700. For the Celtic areas we can point to evidence, running alongside that for all cross-marked stones, that there was an independent tradition of freestanding crosses in another medium. Were Christian graves invariably marked by

115–117 **Stone slabs and crosses** (*Above*) A simple reflection of contemporary wooden crosses? Holm of Noss, Shetland; pre-Viking, probably 7th century. (*Below left*) The mainly Irish development into the recumbent slab: grave-slab of Aigidiu, Durrow, Co. Offaly, late 7th or 8th century. (*Below right*) Partial 'escape' of the shaped cross from the slab, in relief; Gallen Priory, Co. Offaly, Ireland, perhaps late 7th century.

118, 119 **The first High Crosses** (*Above left*) St John's Cross, Iona, Argyll. Reconstruction of this remarkable composite cross, nearly 5 m high, designed and executed in the mid- or late-8th century. (*Above right*) North Cross, Ahenny – a great leap forward in design and execution by a sculptor of genius, perhaps as early as around AD 700.

cross-incised slabs, or were there others (as when the most careful cemetery excavations fail to find stone markers) where 6th-century burials could be indicated by two short bars of wood nailed cross-wise or checked into each other? Certain primary stones do, curiously, seem to depict such wooden crosses. There are later and much more elaborate designs on stone faces – cross-shafts ending in sharp points, cross-arms braced or strutted with diagonals and arcs nailed to the arms – that have been claimed as two-dimensional pictures of composite timber crosses of some size, items certainly well within the capacity of the contemporary woodworking skills. The existence of wooden crosses is mentioned in 7th-century literature – Adomnan implies that, within Columba's lifetime on Iona (563–97), crosses presumably of wood were put up to commemorate an event, and Bede as we saw tells us that in 633 the Northumbrian king Oswald set up, in a dug hole, a cross *facta citato opera* ('made with hasty workmanship') just before his victorious battle at *Hefenfeld*, Heavenfield by the Wall. He adds without comment that it was *de ligno*, 'of wood'. On a late 7th- or early 8th-century Irish stone cross-base, a cleric is quite obviously carrying a composite wooden cross several feet in length.

After about 700, then, specific regional versions of the freestanding stone cross may be supposed. One surprising aspect is the sheer pace of artistic development. Ever-larger and more elaborate forms were produced. The challenge of so much greater a surface area – shaft, head, arms, and now both faces and even the narrower side-surfaces – was promptly taken up. Here, all available spaces could be filled with symmetry and art, not necessarily confined to the strict canon of Christian symbolism. There is no real evidence for the suggestion that some of the most elaborate early High Crosses 'translate' directly in stone an intermediate, composite-timber, construction with decorated metal-work sheets or plates nailed to the surfaces. This step is unnecessary. There is a clear parallelism between the mature art of the metalworker, that of the manuscript illuminator, and the rich relief-sculpture of certain crosses, but the skilled mason must have worked from careful designs on wood or vellum, just as the carvers of 18th- and 19th-century slate headstones are known to have worked from penmanship copybooks. It is also possible that entirely new techniques appeared. Thanks now to Professor Richard Bailey's analysis of Viking-age sculpture in northern England, it can be shown that for intricate panels of interlace, the achievement of symmetry or the matched reversal of designs and the repetition of designs from one monument to another, simple mechanical aids were employed. The mason or the intermediary artist first scratched or chalked around templates and stencils. Sooner or later, all or part of one such template, in leather or sheet-metal, is bound to be recognized from some waterlogged deposit. Given the temper of the age, the existence of separate though matching traditions of metalwork, illumination and sculpture principally under the Church or aristocratic Christian patronage, and the clear witness of rapid technological advances, we can understand how after 700 there was such a rapid efflorescence of the first 'High Crosses'. The inspiration was Irish rather than British. The Ahenny crosses (Co. Tipperary), the packed figure-scene panels on whose bases match at a spatial remove what was happening or would shortly happen on Pictish class II slabs, probably open the catalogue. For Scotland, no less remarkable are the vast and ambitious first Iona crosses, of composite construction. St Oran's Cross (mid- to late 8th-century?) and the related St John's and St Martin's crosses lead, logically, to their numerous later derivatives. The subsequent High Cross traditions, some related to these seminal productions with their complex overall ornamentation, some stemming from different exemplars where summits, terminals and scenic panels were otherwise treated, take us from the 9th to the 12th and even 13th centuries, and into the Middle Ages.

The art of the scribe

The developed, Classical Roman alphabet is among the finest and clearest ever produced; it continues to inspire stone-cutters and typographers. Quite apart from the social standing of Latin and literacy itself, the majestic formal inscriptions of Roman Britain (and, perhaps, even their humble relations the milestones) offered a public standard. We have seen that at a remove this was followed by all Celtic British memorial stones and, because Rome had shown that a statement could be published widely and through time by means other than the spoken voice, the Irish Ogham stones and even the Pictish stones cannot be fully isolated from the effect of Roman lettered notices.

Some sort of literacy was, if not universal, by no means uncommon in late Roman Britain. Many unable to read fully or to speak correct Latin will have known the numerals, or initial abbreviations for commercial substances, or catch-phrases, and Roman cursive – a demotic round-hand – is found in a wide social range. Fifth-century decline will have extinguished most of this, and the intimate connection between spoken Latin alone and the forms of committing Latin alone to Latin writing meant that any retention of writing must have been confined to the Church. The sheet-anchor was, of course, the central and inescapable role of Christian literature (the Bible, psalms and major set sacraments) in correct liturgical worship and in conforming to the correct sequence of the Christian year with its feasts. Expansion – into constructed Easter tables, the annotation of secular events or the record of gifts, ownership and transactions – was secondary but also possible only within the closed world of ecclesiastical literacy. Only here, for example, could written communication from outside be read.

One is moderately confident now that after 400 some hard core of literacy was maintained somewhere in Ireland. Owing its advent to Christianity, not commerce, we must deduce this from Patrick's 5th-century career alone. A telling clue is given by the 'Springmount tablets', from Antrim. To be dated after rather than before 600, this string of wooden plaques, hollow-faced to hold wax for writing exercises, are of entirely Roman descent and had been used to write out Psalms 30 to 32. They take us into the 7th century, a period when Ireland begins to exhibit considerable Christian literacy.

For Celtic Britain the succession is not so easy to detect. It is pointless to adduce the heroic literature which, it is argued, took post-Roman shape in the later British languages: Cumbric in the north (and conceivably P-Celtic Pictish?), early Welsh in the west, even early Cornish in the southwest. Prolonged oral recitals of great men and great doings, of the Otherworld and its larger-than-life denizens, had been practised for centuries. No doubt the dramatic embellishments changed according to taste, but the traditional central narrative was probably maintained by the device of memorizing strings of chanted verse. A written version was not required and the secular literature was not committed to writing before the late first millennium.

Presumably, at still unidentified locales – major churches, or the early monasteries of the 6th century with their schools – there was a British as opposed to Irish literary continuum. Its physical products have not survived. The prepared vellum leaves, the organic inks, the casings, are virtually never represented in any archaeological record. Almost all our samples of cursive writing from Roman Britain are on wood or lead, preserved fortuitously in waterlogged conditions.

The oldest Insular manuscripts are not Celtic British but come from contemporary Ireland. They date from the 7th and 8th centuries and again their preservation follows a combination of accidents, in this case, both historical and geographical. After the 630s Irish clerics and scribes helped to set up and then to staff monastic houses in converted Anglian Northumbria, and during the 7th century Irishmen from Ireland (and Irish and Anglo-Saxon Christians from England) founded fresh monasteries in Europe from the Low Countries to Italy. Because from the late 7th century Northumbria was in enhanced contact with Rome and Europe, and because – unlike the case in Britain or Ireland – many major Continental houses preserved the nuclei of their libraries and scriptoria until the Reformation or later, so, through this network of chance, a few examples of Insular work have come down to us. A very few may have been preserved in Ireland itself through being enshrined, more or less permanently enclosed in a shrine, at comparatively early dates, but

120 A page from the *Cathach* ('St Columba's Psalter', but probably penned after his time).

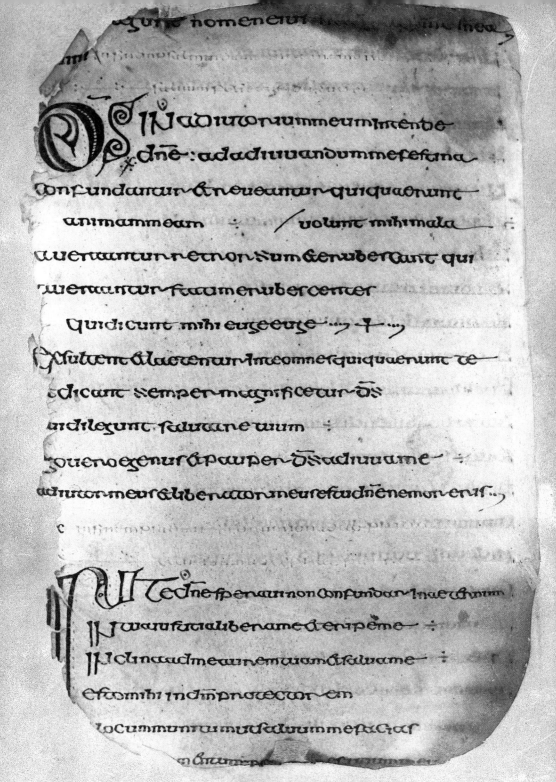

ugustum nomen eius

DS IN adiutorium meum intende
dñe : adadiuuandumme festina
Confundantur & reuereantur quiquaerunt
animam meam / uolunt mihi mala
Auertantur retrorsum & erubescant qui
uolunt mihi mala
Qui dicunt mihi euge euge ⁊
Exultent & laetentur inte omnes qui quaerunt te
dicant semper magnificetur dñs
qui diligunt salutare tuum
Ego uero egenus & pauper dñs adiuuame
adiutor meus & liberator meus es tu dñe ne moreris

N te dñe speraui non confundar inaeternum
In iustitia tua libera me & eripe me
Inclina ad me aurem tuam & salua me
Esto mihi indñm protectorem
& in locum munitum ut saluum me facias

the principal exemplars have (where ascertainable) more complicated histories. The *Cathach* ('St Columba's Psalter', but probably penned after his time) *was* preserved perhaps at Iona and then at Kells in Ireland. It was enshrined in the 11th century, not seen when the shrine went to France after 1691, and discovered when it was returned to Dublin and opened there in 1813. The Book of Durrow, an illuminated Gospel, also enshrined (about 900), escaped the Viking ravages and (minus its lost shrine) was a Cromwellian present to Trinity College, Dublin, in 1661. But there are vital early 7th-century works still in Italy: at Milan, from the monastery at Bobbio founded before 615 by the Irishman Columbanus, and at Florence, where the great Codex Amiatinus of the Vulgate Bible, written and illuminated at Jarrow and/or (Monk)wearmouth before 716 – and hence Northumbrian, artistically Hiberno-Saxon – was sent originally as a gift to Pope Gregory. By the 8th century, other Northumbrian manuscripts could be and were preserved by their religious communities, travelling gradually from house to house in the face of Norse disruptions. Some eventually came, through the hands of noted bibliophiles and collectors in post-Reformation times, to the British Museum (like the Lindisfarne Gospels) or the universities (notably to Corpus Christi College, Cambridge). A similar process in France, in the 18th and 19th centuries, took a mid-8th century copy of Bede's *History* to Leningrad Public Library and an earlier Gospel Book from Echternach (a monastery founded in 698 by Willibrord, an English missionary) to the Bibliothèque Nationale.

Fascinating as these, often imperfectly recorded, provenances may be, we revert to the art. For Christian Celtic Britain in the 5th and 6th centuries, one can do no more than guess that – as with the missing Irish counterparts – there *were* manuscripts as the property of churches and churchmen, that they were plain and probably already in poor condition, and that the hand(s) employed, if the Springmount tablets offer a safe guide, were neither capitals nor cursive but of other kinds. These devolved capital scripts – Insular in Ireland, Uncial in England after St Augustine's arrival in Kent in 597, and variations on both – were gradually subject to enlarged initials, enlarged *decorated* initials and then to illuminated or non-script insertions in or by the actual lines of text. In Ireland, we can take as an instance the small Gospel Book *Codex Usserianus Primus*. This, dating from the start of the 7th century, was either penned in Ireland in imitation of a contemporary imported work or more probably came back to Ireland from somewhere like Bobbio. We deduce, in spite of its damaged state, that individual gospels were divided by non-text pages. The survivor (between *Luke* and *Mark*) has in red and black a tall-stemmed chi-rho dot-outlined between A and W, in a quadrangular border. The Cathach (more certainly Irish) has on the other hand enlarged penmanship initials, and the enlargement into outline also shows the first pictorial terminations: fishy tails, pelta, S-

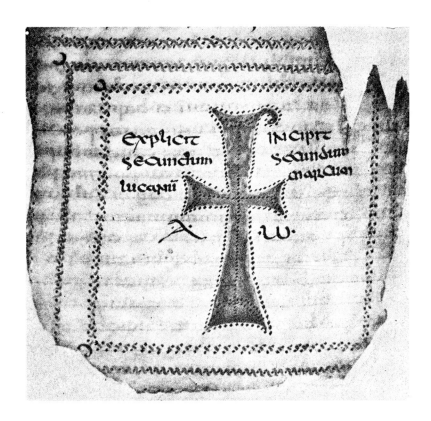

121 The early 7th-century Irish Gospel Book, *Codex Usserianus Primus*: non-text page dividing the Gospels of Luke and Mark, with a tall chi-rho dot-outlined between alpha and omega (A and W).

scroll, stylized opposed bird-heads, a very doggy dolphin, and a small stemmed cross.

There are ample and lavishly illustrated accounts of all the Insular manuscripts readily available and even a condensed précis here would go outside the theme of Celtic Britain and the time-range in question. The artistic parallel is with the art in stone. The extraordinary Insular achievements of the subsequent centuries, the Book of Durrow, the Lindisfarne Gospels, the Book of Kells and others, represent a comparatively rapid and (from a 6th-century viewpoint) unforeseen progress to a stage of applied art, inventiveness and skill in execution far removed from the last days of Roman Britain or sub-Roman times. That stage was similarly attained in superior metalwork and in the first High Crosses, and the stylistic vocabularies are quite obviously related, even interchangeable. *Why* this took place is a question neither history nor archaeology can fully resolve. The long period of Viking incursion disrupted but did not altogether destroy a tradition that, in other forms, reached into the Middle Ages. But it is a matter of argument to what extent the Insular manuscript tradition can really be described either as Celtic, or British.

Epilogue

C ELTIC BRITAIN may in one sense still be with us, but in the sense relevant to this book the post-Roman 'Early Christian Celtic' phase closed during the 8th century AD. Omitting all mention of Ireland's separate and rather different story, we can note how that century saw both the initial dominance of the Anglo-Saxon kingdoms and the first irruptions of the Scandinavian sea-raiders, later to become agrarian settlers, that we usually know as the Vikings. Scotland's internal history is different again, but the same broad period witnessed Vikings in the northern and western Isles, the collation of native Picts and Irish-derived Scots in the north, and a balance between native North Britons and the Northumbrian Angles in the Lowlands and border country. The uneasy pattern of post-Roman days was subjected to a relatively rapid change. In terms of art, of high craftsmanship and of what then passed for architecture the outcome of change was, eventually, impressive. Nevertheless, to take a single category as an instance, high stone crosses with protrusions and piercings, interlace and figure scenes were developed over centuries rather than decades and show the most variegated inspiration. Examples from the west of Scotland, the Isle of Man, south Wales and southwest Britain may well represent and maintain an archaic mode of Christian symbolism, but a great many belong to the 10th, 11th and occasionally even 12th centuries. Formally, they are closer to medieval than to Early Christian sculpture.

If we look back to the 5th century and consider what has been sketched in the foregoing pages, the gaps in our knowledge gradually become patent. Certain questions may never be answered, because the historical evidence is lost for ever and the limitations of archaeology and allied disciplines cannot make good such a loss. If we must still talk about 'the Dark Ages', the darkest patch historically lies somewhere between AD 450 and 600. From the later 6th century we probably enter (for the British) a period of historicity – that is, a time when selected and significant events were recorded in writing, somewhere, reasonably soon after their occurrence and with dates and details we can now partly interpret. From

122 At the end of the Celtic 1st millennium AD. Churchyard cross in granite, Phillack, Cornwall, around AD 1000, in a Christian site that begins in the 5th century. Medieval in type, this simple monument draws on centuries of Celtic British workmanship and successive external inspirations.

the same general horizon we can begin to make sense, archaeologically, of the expansion of Anglo-Saxon settlement and (again for the British, and Irish) of that key component, Christianity in its tangible visible aspect.

Does this not call for *more* archaeology? The answer must be 'Yes', but with reservations that need a brief explanation. Within archaeology, an excavation is not unlike major corrective surgery in the medical world. It cuts out the mass of accumulated evidence. You cannot repeat the operation, even when you realize too late that it could have been better performed, and it is a truism that total excavation of a site spells its total destruction. The climate of opinion today favours exquisitely detailed field survey (which is non-destructive and can be immensely revealing) or fresh analysis, employing new scientific techniques, of the vast quantities of already-excavated finds. Yet very limited excavation, purely for enlightenment and directed only to specific points, both minimizes damage and justifies effort. For Scotland, Professor Leslie Alcock's extremely selective campaign, involving disturbance of only fractions of the areas of key sites where (as precedent suggests) dating material may be expected, has produced information out of all proportion to the expenditure. Concentrating on forts or citadels where documentation points to post-Roman occupation or warfare, his campaign has touched Dumbarton Rock, Dundurn, Dunnottar, Dunollie, Dunragit and Urquhart, not to mention the Pictish palace at Forteviot and the mistakenly identified Northumbrian monastery at St Abb's Head. Comparable schemes of work in Wales and southwest Britain, if planned and executed with matching skills, could hardly fail to offer us matching enlightenment. And on the same topic we have to realize that research excavation on a rather more extended scale is now called for at Tintagel. The nature of both the Celtic British occupation and the richly complex external links at this key site – key to an area stretching beyond Cornwall to Somerset, south Wales and even southwest Ireland – can only be determined archaeologically.

By far the greatest, and hence the most intriguing, problem remains. It, too, may never be resolved and the clarification ultimately rests not with the spade but with another equally old-fashioned resource, the human mind. To revert to a question posed earlier, why am I writing in a language developed from Anglo-Saxon, instead of from Late British Latin or (Celtic) Late British or some amalgam of the two? If we accept the tenor of historical demography that depicts a Britannia, around 400, with three or four million inhabitants, their land invasively settled over the next century and a half by – what shall we suppose? 50,000 or 200,000 Germanic incomers? – must we not still enquire: what happened to all the British? Did they *all* flee west and north, emigrate to Brittany, die of some plague or other or perish at Saxon hands? Very slowly, with growing recourse to such tempting but perhaps misleading analogies as the Romans in North Africa or the British in India, we perceive this to be a, if not *the*, sixty-four million dollar question for the period AD 450–600. Equally slowly we detect a lobby in favour of a modern answer, to the effect that most of the British stayed where they were – in country rather than crumbling town – and in some enigmatic fashion eventually became not Britons at all but Saxons, or Angles, and ultimately English. Naturally between the two extremes of resolution there will lurk an answer, or range of answers reflecting such a process in different parts of Britain. At the moment it is marginally easier to propose some such ethnic and linguistic amalgamation in the North – in Northumbria and Yorkshire – than elsewhere, but the most we ought to claim is that certain approaches (settlement archaeology, place-name study, and a most rigorous reinterpretation of all early historical sources) do appear to be more progressive than others.

It is heartening to report that, in the last years of the 20th century, the whole study of Celtic Britain does at least now proceed on a unitary basis. Nora Chadwick and her husband Professor H. M. Chadwick struggled for years, with gentle but also unrelenting persistence, to show by precept and example that we can no longer parcel out research into tight little compartments, here early Welsh literature, there a Saxon urnfield, up north a Pictish settlement. Mainland Britain, at every stage of its past, is and has been too small a country to suppose that individual discoveries treated in isolation will ever provide more than isolated and localized answers. This book has not been able to stray into the world of the Anglo-Saxons, any more than into Celtic Britain's sister-world of Early Christian Ireland, but at no stage are these other parts of the whole either irrelevant or unnecessary. 'Celtic Britain' is *our* construction, not an entity of time and place perceived by the early inhabitants of the British Isles, Celtic-speaking or otherwise. We overlook that at our peril. The subject-matter has been a glimpse of a few centuries, arbitrarily selected and still most imperfectly perceived. Justification for both the glimpse and the selection can be found, not simply in the intrinsic interest, but in the chance it gives us to appreciate something of the British background. We are no longer concerned with the landgrabbings of the Neolithic period, the fate of ethnic minorities in the Bronze Age or the dynastic squabbles of the pre-Roman Iron Age. But all Britons, and their innumerable descendants overseas, ineluctably continued to share in a Celtic inheritance. It can be no bad thing to wonder how, and why.

Select Bibliography

Chapters 1–3

The British Celtic languages

BROOKS, N., ed. *Latin and the Vernacular Languages in Early Medieval Britain*, Leicester, 1982.

JACKSON, K. H. *Language and History in Early Britain*, Edinburgh, 1953.

– *The Gododdin – The Oldest Scottish Poem*, Edinburgh, 1969.

Place-names

GELLING, M. *Signposts to the Past – Place-Names and the History of England*, London, 1978.

NICOLAISEN, W. H. F. *Scottish Place-Names*, London, 1976.

RIVET, A. L. F., & SMITH, C. C. *The Place-Names of Roman Britain*, London, 1979.

Late Roman Britain

CASEY, P. J., ed. *The End of Roman Britain*, Oxford (BAR 71), 1979.

COLLINGWOOD, R. G., & WRIGHT, R. P. *The Roman Inscriptions of Britain*, vol. I, Inscriptions on Stone, Oxford, 1965.

FRERE, S. S. *Britannia: A History of Roman Britain*, rev. edn., London, 1978.

OGILVIE, R. M., & RICHMOND, (Sir) Ian, eds., *Cornelii Taciti; De Vita Agricolae*, Oxford, 1967.

SALWAY, P. *The Frontier People of Roman Britain*, Cambridge, 1965.

– *Roman Britain*, Oxford, 1981.

Paganism

ROSS, A. *Pagan Celtic Britain*, London, 1967.

English conquests

ARNOLD, C. J. *Roman Britain to Saxon England*, London and Sydney, 1984.

CAMPBELL, J., ed. *The Anglo-Saxons*, London, 1982.

HUNTER BLAIR, P. *Northumbria in the Days of Bede*, London, 1976.

MYRES, J. N. L. *The English Settlements*, Oxford, 1986.

Gildas

LAPIDGE, M., & DUMVILLE, D., eds. *Gildas: New Approaches* (= Studies in Celtic History, V), Woodbridge, 1984.

O'SULLIVAN, T. D. *The De Excidio of Gildas – Its Authenticity and Date*, Leiden (E. J. Brill), 1978.

WINTERBOTTOM, M., ed. *Gildas. The Ruin of Britain and other works* (Arthurian Period Sources no. 7), Chichester, 1978.

Mediterranean imports

THOMAS, C. 'Imported Late-Roman Mediterranean Pottery in Ireland and Western Britain; chronologies and implications', *Proc. Royal Irish Academy*, series C, 76, 1976, 245–256.

– *A Provisional List of Imported Pottery in Post-Roman Western Britain & Ireland*, Redruth (Institute of Cornish Studies, spec. rep. 7), 1981.

General studies

ALCOCK, L. *Arthur's Britain – History and Archaeology AD 367–634*, Harmondsworth and Baltimore, 1971 (paperback edn. 1973).

– *'By South Cadbury is that Camelot . . .' – Excavations at Cadbury Castle 1966–70*, London, 1972.

BOWEN, E. G. *Britain and the Western Seaways*, London and New York, 1972 (chaps. 5 to 8).

CHADWICK, N. K., ed. *Studies in the Early British Church*, Cambridge, 1958.

– *Studies in Early British History*, Cambridge, 1959.

LAING, L. *The Archaeology of Late Celtic Britain and Ireland, c.400–1200 AD*, London, 1975.

THOMAS, C. *Christianity in Roman Britain to AD 500*, London, 1981.

Chapter 4 Early Cornwall

General history

ELLIOTT-BINNS, L. E. *Medieval Cornwall*, London, 1955.

HALLIDAY, F. E. *A History of Cornwall*, London, 1959.

PEARCE, S. M. *The Kingdom of Dumnonia – Studies in History and Tradition in South Western Britain AD 350–1150*, Padstow, 1978.

General archaeology

FOX, (Lady) A. *South West England 3500 BC–AD 600*, Newton Abbot, 1973, chaps. 8 & 9.

PEARCE, S. M. *The Archaeology of South West Britain*, London, 1981, chaps. 4 & 5.

Roman impact

BRANIGAN, K., & FOWLER, P. J., eds. *The Roman West Country*, Newton Abbot, 1976.

THOMAS, C. 'The Character and Origins of Roman Dumnonia', in C. Thomas, ed., *Rural Settlement in Roman Britain*, London, 1966, 74–98.

Language and Place-Names

ELLIS, P. B. *The Cornish Language and Its Literature*, London, 1974.

PADEL, O. J. *Cornish Place-Name Elements* (English Place-Name Society, vol. 56/57), Nottingham, 1985.

Isles of Scilly

ASHBEE, P. *Ancient Scilly – From the First Farmers to the Early Christians*, Newton Abbot, 1974.

THOMAS, C. *Exploration of a Drowned Landscape – Archaeology and History of the Isles of Scilly*, London, 1985.

Tintagel and early legendary material

BURROW, I. C. G. 'Tintagel – Some Problems', in *Scottish Archaeological Forum 5 1973*, Edinburgh, 1974, 99–103.

DARK, K. R. 'The Plan and Interpretation of Tintagel', *CMCS* no. 9, 1985, 1–18.

PADEL, O. J. 'The Cornish Background of the Tristan Stories', *CMCS* no. 1, 1981, 1–20.

– 'Geoffrey of Monmouth and Cornwall', *CMCS* no. 8, 1984, 1–28.

THOMAS, C. 'East and West: Tintagel, Mediterranean Imports and the Early Insular Church', in S. M. Pearce, ed. *The Early Church in Western Britain and Ireland*, Oxford (BAR Brit. ser. 102), 1982, 17–34.

– *Tintagel Castle* (English Heritage guide), London, 1986.

Stone crosses

LANGDON, A. G. *Old Cornish Crosses*, Truro and London, 1896.

Christianity

See under Chapter 7.

Chapter 5 Early Scotland

General history

BARROW, G. W. S. *The Kingdom of the Scots*, London, 1973.

DONALDSON, G. *Scottish Kings* (2nd edn.), London, 1977.

HANHAM, H. J. *Scottish Nationalism*, London, 1969.

SMOUT, T. C. *A History of the Scottish People 1560–1830*, London, 1969.

SMYTH, A. P. *Warlords and Holy Men – Scotland AD 80–1000*, London, 1984.

General archaeology

RITCHIE, G. & A. *Scotland – Archaeology and Early History*, London, 1981.

Roman impact

BREEZE, D. J. & DOBSON, B. *Hadrian's Wall*, Harmondsworth and Baltimore, 1976.

HANSON, W. & MAXWELL, G. *Rome's North West Frontier – The Antonine Wall*, Edinburgh, 1983.

RICHMOND, I. A., ed. *Roman and Native in North Britain*, Edinburgh and London, 1958.

The Picts

ALCOCK, L. 'Populi Bestiales Pictorum Feroci Animo – A Survey of Pictish Settlement Archaeology', in W. Hanson & L. Keppie, eds., *Roman Frontier Studies 1979*, 61–95, Oxford (BAR Internat. ser. 71), 1980.

ALLEN, J. R. & ANDERSON, J. *The Early Christian Monuments of Scotland*, Edinburgh, 1903 [contains all Pictish stones to date].

HENDERSON, I. *The Picts*, London and New York, 1967.

FRIZELL, J. G. P. & WATSON, W. G., eds. *Pictish Studies – Settlement, Burial and Art in Dark Age Northern Britain*, Oxford (BAR Internat. ser. 125), 1984.

MACGREGOR, M. *Early Celtic Art in North Britain*, 2 vols., Leicester, 1976.

WAINWRIGHT, F. T., ed. *The Problem of the Picts*, Edinburgh and London, 1955.

WAINWRIGHT, F. T. *The Souterrains of Southern Pictland*, London, 1963.

Dalriadic Scots

BANNERMAN, J. *Studies in the History of Dalriada*, Edinburgh and London, 1974.

North Britons

JACKSON, K. H. (and others) *Celt and Saxon – Studies in the Early British Border*, Cambridge, 1963.

JACKSON, K. H. *The Gododdin, The Oldest Scottish Poem*, Edinburgh, 1969.

TOLSTOY, N. *The Quest for Merlin*, London, 1985.

Place-Names

NICOLAISEN, W. F. H. *Scottish Place-Names*, London, 1976.

WATSON, W. J. *The History of the Celtic Place-Names of Scotland*, Edinburgh and London, 1926.

Christianity

See under Chapter 7.

Chapter 6 Early Wales

General history

BOWEN, E. G. *The Settlements of the Celtic Saints in Wales*, Cardiff, 1954.

DAVIES, W. *Wales in the Early Middle Ages*, Leicester, 1982.

JONES, G. R. J. 'Post-Roman Wales', in H. P. R. Finberg, ed., *The Agrarian History of England & Wales, Vol. I. ii, AD 43–1042*, 283–384, Cambridge, 1972.

MOORE, D., ed. *The Irish Sea Province in Archaeology and History*, Cardiff (Cambrian Archaeol. Assoc.), 1972.

REES, W. *An Historical Atlas of Wales, From Early to Modern Times*, new edn., London, 1959.

WILLIAMS, A. H. *An Introduction to the History of Wales; I (Prehistoric Times to 1063 AD)*, Cardiff, 1962.

General archaeology

HOULDER, C. *Wales – An Archaeological Guide*, London, 1974.

STANFORD, S. C. *The Archaeology of the Welsh Marches*, London, 1980.

Roman impact

RCAHMW (Royal Commission on Ancient & Historical Monuments in Wales) *Glamorgan, Vol. I: Pre-Norman, Pt. II, The Iron Age and Roman Occupation*, Cardiff, 1976.

NASH-WILLIAMS, V. E. *The Roman Frontier in Wales*, 2nd edn., Cardiff, 1969.

Inscribed stones & early crosses

NASH-WILLIAMS, V. E. *The Early Christian Monuments of Wales*, Cardiff, 1950.

Post-Roman sites & monuments

ALCOCK, L. *Dinas Powys – An Iron Age, Dark Age and Early Medieval Settlement in Glamorgan*, Cardiff, 1963.

FOSTER, I. LL. & DANIEL, G. E., eds. *Prehistoric and Early Wales*, London, 1965 (chaps. 6, 7, 8).

MOORE, D., ed. *The Land of Dyfed in Early Times*, Cardiff (Cambrian Archaeol. Assoc.), 1964.

RCAHMW *Glamorgan, Vol. I: Pt. III, The Early Christian Period*, Cardiff, 1976.

SAVORY, H. N. 'Excavations at Dinas Emrys, Beddgelert (Caerns.), 1954–6', *Archaeologia Cambrensis*, 109, 1960, 13–77.

WAINWRIGHT, G. J. *Coygan Camp, a Prehistoric, Romano-British and Dark Age Settlement in Carmarthenshire*, Cardiff, 1977.

Irish in Wales

RICHARDS, M. 'Irish settlements in south-west Wales, a topographical approach', *Journ. Roy. Soc. Antiquaries Ireland*, 90, 1960, 133–162.

THOMAS, C. 'Irish settlements in post-Roman Western Britain,' *Journ. Roy. Institution Cornwall*, n.s. 6, 1972, 251–274.

Early Welsh literature and society

BARTRUM, P. C., ed. *Early Welsh Genealogical Tracts*, Cardiff, 1966.

BROMWICH, R. *Trioedd Ynys Prydein – The Welsh Triads*, Cardiff, 1961.

DAVIES, W. *An Early Welsh Microcosm – Studies in the Llandaff Charters*, London (Roy. Historical Soc.), 1978.

– *The Llandaff Charters*, Aberystwyth (Nat. Library Wales), 1979.

JENKINS, D., & OWEN, M. E., eds. *The Welsh Law of Women*, Cardiff, 1980.

MILLER, M. *The Saints of Gwynedd* (= Studies in Celtic History, I), Woodbridge, 1979.

WADE-EVANS, A. W. *Vitae Sanctorum Britanniae et Genealogiae*, Cardiff, 1944.

Christianity

See under Chapter 7.

Offa's Dyke

FOX, C. *Offa's Dyke – a field survey, etc.*, London (British Academy), 1955.

The Welsh overseas

WILLIAMS, Glyn *The Desert and the Dream*, Cardiff, 1975.

WILLIAMS, Gwyn A. *The Search for Beulah Land*, London, 1980.
WILLIAMS, R. B. *Y Wladfa*, Cardiff, 1975.

Chapter 7 Church and Monastery

General studies

BARLEY, M. W., & HANSON, R. P. C., eds. *Christianity in Britain, 300–700*, Leicester, 1968.
CHADWICK, N. K. *The Age of the Saints in the Early Celtic Church* (Riddell Memorial Lectures, Durham, 1960), Oxford, 1961.
HENIG, M. *Religion in Roman Britain*, London, 1984.
HUGHES, K. *Celtic Britain in the Early Middle Ages* (= Studies in Celtic History, II), Woodbridge, 1980.
MACQUEEN, J. *St. Nynia, a study of literary and linguistic evidence*, Edinburgh and London, 1961.
RCAHMS (Royal Commission on the Ancient & Historical Monuments of Scotland) *The Outer Hebrides, Skye & The Small Isles*, Edinburgh, 1928.
– *Orkney and Shetland* (3 vols.: Report & Intro., Orkney, Shetland) Edinburgh, 1946.
– *Argyll, Vol. 4: Iona*, Edinburgh, 1982.
SCOTTISH ARCHAEOLOGICAL FORUM No. 5 1973, *Problems of Celtic and Northern English Monastic Settlements* (various authors), Edinburgh, 1974.
THOMAS, C. *The Early Christian Archaeology of North Britain*, Oxford, 1971.
– *Christianity in Roman Britain to AD 500*, London, 1981 (2nd edn., new intro., 1985).
VICTORY, S. *The Celtic Church in Wales*, London, 1977.
WILLIAMS, H. *Christianity in Early Britain*, Oxford, 1912.

The major Roman hoards

KENT, J. P. C., & PAINTER, K. S. *Wealth of the Roman World – Gold and Silver AD 300–700*, London (British Museum), 1977.
PAINTER, K. S. *The Water Newton Early Christian Silver*, London (British Museum), 1977.
JOHNS, C., & POTTER, T. W. *The Thetford Treasure*, London (British Museum), 1983.

Germanus and Patrick

THOMPSON, E. A. *Saint Germanus of Auxerre and the End of Roman Britain* (= Studies in Celtic History, VI), Woodbridge, 1984.
BIELER, L. *The Life and Legend of Saint Patrick*, Dublin, 1948.

HANSON, R. P. C. *Saint Patrick: His Origins and Career*, Oxford, 1968.
– *Saint-Patrick, Confession et Lettre à Coroticus*, Paris ('Sources Chrétiennes', Les Éditions du Cerf), 1978.
HOOD, A. B. E. *St. Patrick, His Writings and Muirchu's Life*, Chichester (Arthurian Period Sources no. 9: Phillimore), 1978.

Alban and Augustine

MORRIS, J. 'The date of St Alban', *Hertfordshire Archaeologist*, I, 1968, 1–8.
RUNCIE, R., ed. *Cathedral and City – St Albans ancient and modern*, St Albans, 1977.
SWINSON, A. *The Quest for Alban*, St Albans, 1970.
BROOKS, N. *The Early History of the Church of Canterbury*, Leicester, 1984 (chap. 1).
COLGRAVE, B., & MYNORS, R. A. B., eds. *Bede's Ecclesiastical History of the English People*, Oxford, 1969.
MASON, A. J. *The Mission of St Augustine to England, etc.*, Cambridge, 1897.
PLUMMER, C., ed. *Venerabilis Baedae Opera Historica* (orig. 2 vols, 1896), single vol., Oxford, 1946.

Inscribed memorial stones

JACKSON, K. H. *Language and History in Early Britain*, Edinburgh, 1954 (chap. V).
MACALISTER, R. A. S. *Corpus Inscriptionum Insularum Celticarum, Vol. I*, Dublin (Stationery Office), 1945.
NASH-WILLIAMS, V. E. *The Early Christian Monuments of Wales*, Cardiff, 1950.

Burials and shrines

PRESTON-JONES, A. 'The Excavation of a Long-Cist Cemetery at Carnanton, St Mawgan, 1943', *Cornish Archaeology*, 23, 1984, 157–178.
COWIE, T. G. 'Excavations at the Catstane, Midlothian, 1977', *Proc. Soc. Antiquaries Scotland*, 109, 1977–78, 166–201.
SMALL, A., THOMAS, C. & WILSON, D. M. *St Ninian's Isle and Its Treasure*, 2 vols. (= Aberdeen Univ. Studies 152), Oxford, 1973.
THOMAS, C. 'An Early Christian Cemetery & Chapel on Ardwall Isle, Kirkcudbright', *Medieval Archaeology*, 11, 1967, 127–188
– 'Lundy, 1969', *Current Archaeology*, no. 16, Sept. 1969, 138–142.

Chapter 8 Art

Prehistoric Celtic art

DIRECTION DES MUSEES DE FRANCE *L'Art Celtique*

en Gaule, 1983–84 (illus. exhibition vol.), Marseille-Paris-Bordeaux-Dijon, 1983.

Fox, (Sir) Cyril *Pattern and Purpose – A Survey of Celtic Art in Britain*, Cardiff (Nat. Museum Wales).

MEGAW, J. V. S. *Art of the European Iron Age*, Bath, 1970.

Coinage as art

ALLEN, D. F. (ed. NASH, D.) *The Coins of the Ancient Celts*, Edinburgh, 1980.

Early metalwork

FOWLER, E. 'Celtic Metalwork of the 5th–6th centuries AD, a re-appraisal', *Archaeol. Journal*, 120, 1964, 98–160.
– 'The origin and development of the penannular brooch in Europe', *Proc. Prehist. Soc.*, 26, 1960, 149–177.

HASELOFF, G. 'Fragments of a hanging bowl from Bekesbourne, Kent, and some ornamental problems,' *Medieval Archaeology*, 2, 1958, 72–103.

HAWKES, S. C. 'A Late Roman Buckle from Tripontium', *Trans. Birmingham Warwickshire Archaeol. Soc.*, 85, 1973, 146–159.

HAWKES, S. C., & DUNNING, G. C. 'Soldiers and Settlers in Britain 4th to 5th Century', *Medieval Archaeology*, 5, 1961, 1–70.

HENRY, F. 'Hanging bowls', *Journ. Roy. Soc. Antiquaries Ireland*, 66, 1936, 209–310.
– 'Irish Enamels of the Dark Ages (etc.)', in D. B. HARDEN, ed., *Dark-Age Britain*, London, 1956, 71–90.

KENDRICK, T. D. *Anglo-Saxon Art to AD 900*, London, 1938 (repr. 1972).

KILBRIDE-JONES, H. *Zoomorphic Penannular Brooches*, London (= Soc. of Antiquaries Res. Report 39), 1980.

LEEDS, E. T. *Celtic ornament in the British Isles down to AD 700*, Oxford, 1933.
– *Early Anglo-Saxon Art and Archaeology*, Oxford, 1936.

SMALL, A., THOMAS, C., & WILSON, D. M. *St Ninian's Isle and Its Treasure*, 2 vols. (= Aberdeen Univ. studies, 152), Oxford, 1973.

STEVENSON, R. B. K. 'The Hunterston Brooch and Its Significance', *Medieval Archaeology*, 18, 1974, 16–42.

Pictish art and its background

ANDERSON, J., & ALLEN, J. R. *The Early Christian Monuments of Scotland*, Edinburgh (Soc. of Antiquaries of Scotland), 1903.

FRIELL, J. G. P., & WATSON, W. G., eds. *Pictish Studies*, Oxford (BAR Internat. ser. 125), 1984.

HENDERSON, I. M. *The Picts*, London, 1967.
– 'The Silver Chain from Whitecleuch . . . Lanarkshire', *Trans. Dumfries & Galloway Natur. Hist. & Antiq. Soc.*, 54, 1979, 20–28.

JACKSON, A. *The Symbol Stones of Scotland*, Kirkwall (Orkney Press), 1984.

MORRIS, R. W. B. *The Prehistoric Rock Art of Argyll*, Poole, 1977.
– *The Prehistoric Rock Art of Galloway and the Isle of Man*, Poole, 1979.
– *The Prehistoric Rock Art of Southern Scotland*, Oxford (BAR Brit. ser. 86), 1981.

STEVENSON, R. B. K. 'Pictish Art', in F. T. WAINWRIGHT, ed., *The Problem of the Picts*, Edinburgh & London, 1955, 97–128.

THOMAS, C. 'The Animal Art of the Scottish Iron Age and Its Origins', *Archaeol. Journal*, 118, 1961, 14–64.
– 'The Pictish Class I Symbol Stones', in J. G. P. FRIELL & W. G. WATSON, eds., *Pictish Studies*, 1984, 169–188.

Beginnings of Insular sculpture

HENRY, F. *Irish Art in the Early Christian Period to AD 800*, London, rev. edn., 1965.

Manuscript art

ALEXANDER, J. J. G. *Insular Manuscripts, 6th to the 9th century*, London, 1979.

LOWE, E. A. *English Uncial*, Oxford, 1960.

Epilogue

L. Alcock's campaign

ALCOCK, L. 'Early Historic Fortifications in Scotland', in G. Guilbert (ed.), *Hillfort Studies*, 150–201, Leicester, 1981.
– 'Gwyr y Gogledd: An Archaeological Appraisal', *Archaeologia Cambrensis*, vol. 132 (1983), 1–18.
– 'The Archaeology of Celtic Britain, Fifth to Twelfth Centuries A.D.', in D. A. Hinton (ed.), *25 Years of Medieval Archaeology*, 48–66, Sheffield, 1983.

The problem of British survival

FAULL, M. 'British Survival in Anglo-Saxon Northumbria', in L. Laing (ed.), *Studies in Celtic Survival*, 1–56, Oxford, (BAR 37), 1977.

THOMAS, C. *Christianity in Roman Britain to AD 500*, London, 1981, chap. 10 with maps.

JACKSON, K. H. 'Angles and Britons in Northumbria and Cumbria', in H. Lewis (ed.), *Angles and Britons – O'Donnell Lectures*, Cardiff, 1963, 60–84.

CHADWICK, N. K. 'The British or Celtic Part in the Population of England', *ibidem*, 110–147.

Abbreviation *CMCS* = *Cambridge Medieval Celtic Studies*

A note on sources

Final excavation reports on many sites mentioned, and on future relevant sites, may appear anywhere within a huge range of national or local archaeological journals; or even in Council for British Archaeology regional-group publications or the bulletins of local research groups. The non-specialist reader does, however, have various cumulative annual abstracts, in which topics can be sought by subject or locality. The CBA (Council for British Archaeology) *Archaeological Bibliography for Great Britain and Ireland* – up to 1979 – has now been largely replaced by the *CBA British Archaeological Abstracts* (from 1968). The fullest chronicle of work in progress for the period is compiled annually in *Medieval Archaeology* (Society for Medieval Archaeology, London). Since 1971, a certain amount of 5th-century matter is included, alongside that of the 1st to 4th centuries, in the annual *Britannia* (Society for the Promotion of Roman Studies, London).

List of Illustrations

Unless otherwise credited, photographs and drawings are by the author. The abbreviation 'RIB' indicates drawings after R. G. Collingwood and R. P. Wright, *Roman Inscriptions of Britain*, vol. I, *Inscriptions on Stone*, Oxford, 1965. 'Macalister' refers to R. A. S. Macalister, *Corpus Inscriptionum Insularum Celticarum*, vol. I, Dublin, 1945.

Index